P9-EKC-605

the crafter's
P R O J E C T   B O O K

80+ PROJECTS TO MAKE AND DECORATE

MARY ANN HALL   SANDRA SALAMONY

Copyright © 2000 by
Rockport Publishers, Inc.

All rights reserved. No part of this book may be
reproduced in any form without written permission
of the copyright owners. All images in this book
have been reproduced with the knowledge and
prior consent of the artists concerned and no
responsibility is accepted by producer, publisher, or
printer for any infringement of copyright or other-
wise, arising from the contents of this publication.
Every effort has been made to ensure that credits
accurately comply with information supplied.

First published in the
United States of America by
Rockport Publishers, Inc.
33 Commercial Street
Gloucester, Massachusetts 01930-5089
Telephone: (978) 282-9590
Facsimile: (978) 283-2742
www.rockpub.com

ISBN 1-56496-594-5

10 9 8 7 6 5 4 3 2 1

Design: Leeann Leftwich

All photography by Kevin Thomas except for
photographs on the following pages, used by
permission from *Handcraft Illustrated:*
pgs. 39, 53, 82, 93, 108, 110, 128, 142

Printed in China.

PUBLISHER'S NOTE
The projects shown in the *Crafter's Project Book* offer
many new craft ideas, using a variety of mediums.
Always use caution when working with paint, glass,
metal, or chemicals. Make sure your work area is
well-ventilated and wear protective eye gear,
gloves, and a respirator. Follow the manufacturer's
safety instructions, and keep chemicals and other
toxic substances well out of the reach of children.
The author and publisher do not accept any liablity
for any accidents.

contents

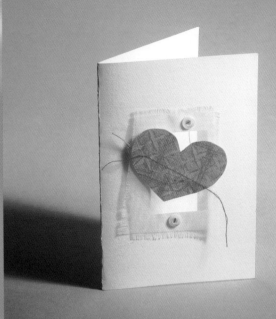

introduction

In *The Crafter's Project Book,* recipes from *The Crafter's Recipe Book* are used to create dazzling projects for decorating and gift-giving. *The Crafter's Recipe Book,* by Jessica Wrobel (Rockport Publishers, 1998), contains a wonderful collection of over 100 "recipes" for creating unique effects on paper, fabric, glass, metal, and ceramic surfaces. That book has quickly become a favorite resource for crafters and artists alike. The overwhelming response to the "recipe" book demanded an equally exciting follow-up, hence the book you have in front of you.

The Crafter's Project Book gathers together an array of projects from cards, books, journals, coasters, place mats, candles, candle holders, frames, chimes, glassware, pillows, lampshades, scarves, jewelry, and much more. Whether you're looking for a creative way to spend a quiet Saturday or to share fun ideas with your friends or your children, this book offers much inspiration. From something as simple as making glitter-coated candles to layering hand-made postcards with old dress patterns, the projects in this book will delight the dabbler, the enthusiast, and the serious (or not serious!) artist.

Curating this book was a bit like being on a treasure hunt. I was continually surprised and inspired by the submissions from this excellent pool of artists, many of whom I've worked with in the past, and many whose work I discovered during frequent jaunts to galleries and craft shows over the last year. Their works are not merely beautiful. To me, they each have a little something special. Whether that extra something is wit, elegance, ingenuity, simplicity, glamour, currency, or humor—-it's the quality that brings a project to life and holds it together. Perhaps it's the glimmer of the personality that created it, or simply "good design." It's that charm that only handmade items possess. I know it when I see it. You probably do too. I hope you are as charmed by these projects as I was. And I hope these ideas urge you on to explore and indulge your own creative impulses. Enjoy!

Mary Ann Hall

basics

You'll need to have a few general craft supplies handy to complete most of the projects featured in this book: a craft knife and cutting board, for example; as well as scissors; a ruler or triangle; low-tack masking tape; sponges; fine- and medium-grit sandpaper; and, of course, foam paint brushes. Common household accessories should be available, including rubbing alcohol and cotton balls, tweezers, measuring cups, and glass cleaner. It's also assumed that you'll have access to basic household appliances such as a kitchen timer, a washing machine and dryer, or an iron and ironing board.

When beginning a project, take a tip from architects and graphic designers and sketch your preliminary design ideas on tracing paper or vellum. First, trace the outline of the surface at 100% on transparent paper. Then, sketch your designs within the outline and transfer your final choice to the project surface. You can also use a traced template to arrange mosaic pieces, collage items, or decoupage papers before gluing them to the prepared base.

Patterns for many of the projects are provided at the end of the book, beginning on page 162. There are many techniques for transferring these images to your work in progress. One simple method is to trace the design onto transparent vellum or tracing paper using a #1 pencil. With low-tack masking tape, secure the paper, image-side down, onto the project surface, and re-trace the lines firmly with a ballpoint pen to transfer the image. Note that this will result in a mirror image of the original design.

Transfer embossing lines directly onto metal surfaces by securing the photocopy or sketched image to the metal with tape and tracing the outlines with a ballpoint pen or an awl.

To transfer a cutting outline, lightly spray the back of a photocopied pattern with re-positionable spray adhesive, place it on the project surface, and cut along the template guidelines, removing the paper when finished. If you don't have access to a well-ventilated area to use the spray adhesive, position the photocopy over the craft material and poke holes with a straight pin through both layers at corners and other important points; remove the paper and use the pinholes as a cutting guide.

And, of course, you can always use chalk, good old carbon paper, or colored sewing tracing paper to transfer patterns and drawing lines to projects.

Finally, don't forget basic safety issues. Some of the materials used in these projects are caustic; wear rubber gloves when applying them. Wear protective eyeglasses and leather gloves when working with metal foils and wires or when nipping tile or other ceramic pieces. And always work in a well-ventilated area and wear a respirator when toxic fumes are present.

Refer to the *Crafter's Recipe Book* for many other paper, fabric, and metal treatments that you can adapt to use with the projects featured here. But most of all, remember to have fun and let your creativity shine!

paper projects

ARTIST: SUSAN JAWORSKI-STRANC

MATERIALS

• 3-ply chipboard or mat board
  for book covers: 6 pieces
  7 1/4" x 5 3/4" (18.5 cm x 15 cm)
  and 6 pieces 1 1/4" x 5 3/4"
  (3.5 cm x 15 cm)
  for wrapper supports: 1 piece
  8 3/4" x 2 1/4" (22 cm x 7 cm)
  and 1 piece 8 3/4" x 1 1/4"
  (22 cm x 3.5 cm)

• Paste paper (see page 13)
  for book covers: 6 pieces
  7 1/4" x 6 1/4" (18.5 cm x 15.5 cm)
  for wrapper: 1 piece 19" x 9 1/2"
  (48 cm x 24 cm)

• Decorative paper
  for book cover lining: 6 pieces
  8 1/2" x 5 1/2" (22 cm x 14 cm)
  for book spines: 6 pieces 7" x 3"
  (18 cm x 8 cm)
  for wrapper lining: 1 piece
  17" x 8 3/4" (43 cm x 22 cm)

• 90 sheets of 8 1/2" x 5 1/2"
  stationery (22 cm x 14 cm)
• artist tape
• PVA glue
• 24" (61 cm) leather lace
• single-eye button
• 1/4" (.5 cm) hole punch
• 2 yards 1/8" to 1/4" (.32 cm to
  .5 cm) wide ribbon

Organize your collection of personal memoirs, nature studies, or traveler's notes in this handsome group of handmade books. A special gift for mothers-to-be, writers, or anyone interested in scrapbooks, these journals and their matching wrapper are constructed from decorative paste paper that you make yourself. They are a perfect shower gift for a bride-to-be—she can use one book as a guest book, another for special wedding photographs, and the final as a scrapbook of the event.

paste-paper journals
with matching wrapper

Makes three 30-page books and coordinating wrapper

Book Construction

1 Attach a 7 1/4" x 5 3/4" (18.5 cm x 15 cm) piece of mat board to a 1 1/4" x 5 3/4" (3.5 cm x 15 cm) piece with artist's tape, leaving a 1/2" (1 cm) gap between the boards to create the hinged book cover frame. Repeat for back cover.

2 Bond paste paper to the outside of the book cover pieces with PVA glue. Glue one piece of the 7" x 3" (18 cm x 8 cm) decorative spine paper to each cover piece, overlapping the hinged end. Fold corners diagonally to the inside of the covers and glue, pressing firmly to adhere. Fold and glue paper edges to the inside of the covers. Glue a piece of 8 1/2" x 5 1/2" cover lining to the inside of each cover. Using a hole punch, create three evenly spaced binding holes through the smaller hinged piece of each cover.

3 Assemble 30 pages of the 8 1/2" x 5 1/2" (22 cm x 14 cm) stationery to create the book block. Using the paper hole punch and the holes of the book cover spine as a guide, pierce the sheets a few pages at a time. With the ribbon and needle, lace together covers and pages using Japanese stab binding or a pamphlet stitch, knotting at the back of the center hole.

4 Repeat to create two additional books.

Wrapper Construction

1 Using PVA glue, adhere the two wrapper support boards to the wrong side of the wrapper lining at opposite short ends of the paper. Then, center and bond the wrong side of the liner (with supports) to the wrong side of the 19" x 9 1/2" (48 cm x 24 cm) paste paper wrapper piece. Fold over paste paper edges and glue to inside wrapper lining.

2 With the hole punch, make a hole at the center of the larger support board. Knot one end of the leather lace and thread the other end through a button. Pull until button is secure up against the knot. Take the unknotted end of the leather and pull it through the hole in the wrapper from the outside until button is flush against paste paper. Knot end of lace.

Finalizing the Collection

Stack all three books in the inside center of wrapper. Fold the plain wrapper end over books and then fold over the side with the leather lace. Draw the leather piece around the outside of the wrapper and books until it meets the button. Twist leather lace around button to secure.

VARIATION

Use drawing paper instead of stationery for the inside pages and turn the journals into sketchbooks.

Paste Paper Recipe

The paste-paper technique described here is similar to print-making, but you can also "finger-paint" with the translucent flour paste directly on the paper for unique designs.

MATERIALS
- 12 sheets 18" x 24" (46 cm x 61 cm) high-quality drawing paper
- 5 tablespoons all-purpose flour
- 4 tablespoons rice flour
- 3 cups cold water
- 1 teaspoon liquid dishwashing detergent
- craft acrylics, any six colors
- 20" x 26" (51 cm x 66 cm) acrylic sheet
- Assorted graining, stamping, and drawing tools
- general craft supplies

Makes twelve 18" x 24" (46 cm x 61 cm) sheets of paste paper

1 Whisk the two flours together in a 2-quart saucepan and moisten with a little of the cold water. Add the remaining water and continue to whisk until the mixture is smooth and free of lumps. Stirring constantly, cook over medium heat until almost boiling. The paste will begin to thicken at this point. Reduce the heat and cook for 1–2 minutes more. Remove from heat and stir in the liquid detergent.

2 Spoon about 1/2 cup of paste into six disposable containers such as yogurt cups and reserve the remainder. Add acrylic paint to each container until desired color is achieved, and stir well.

3 Over a washable surface, create your design on the acrylic sheet by spreading the colored paste evenly using a wide, flat brush or the edge of your hand. Manipulate the paste with your fingers, the edge of your hand, a tool, or a foam stamp to create a design. Try repeating motifs at regular intervals for graphic interest.

4 Place the blank drawing paper onto the acrylic sheet, starting from one edge, and stroke the back of the paper to transfer your design. Lift the paper off the acrylic sheet and lay flat.

5 Repeat steps 3 and 4 for each print, adding paste as needed. Additional colors can be overprinted by cleaning acrylic sheet, designing a pattern with the new color of paste, and printing on the paper while the previous layer of paste is still wet. When finished, dry the paper flat overnight, then press on the wrong side using dry, low-heat iron to smooth.

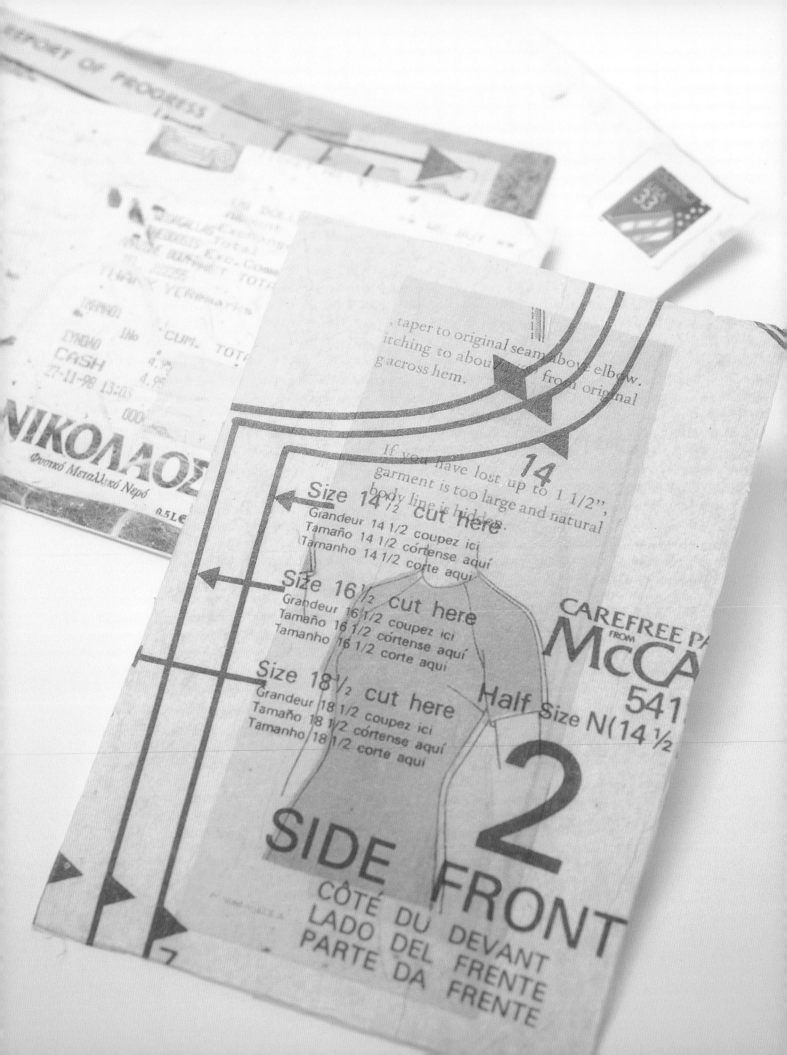

The choice of a postcard can reveal more about the sender than any other form of communication. These collage cards feature recycled dress patterns layered with other found materials. Design the cards with thematic items for a cohesive look, or let cards be random expressions of color, texture, and originality. Add multiple layers of tissue paper to add depth as well as tone, and consider tearing the edges for a rough, distressed appearance. Don't be afraid to over-wrinkle the paper; it will add to the aged look of the final piece.

dress-pattern
postcards

Makes unlimited postcards

1 Arrange collage items on a blank postcard, then glue into place.

2 Layer tissue paper or other see-through papers such as dress patterns. Glue into place. Sand through top layer in random places to distress if desired. Let dry overnight.

3 Apply random patches of bronze leaf according to manufacturer's recommendations if so desired.

4 Trim edges with scissors or craft knife. Cut to postcard size if necessary. If the postcard curls after it is dry, layer the card between sheets of wax paper and press under heavy books for at least 12 hours.

VARIATION
Tint the final card with brewed tea to further enhance the vintage appearance.

MATERIALS
• 4" x 6" blank postcards
• PVA glue or wallpaper paste
• collage materials:
  postage stamps, tags from mer-
  chandise, rice paper, vintage
  handwriting samples, handmade
  paper, wrapping paper, old maps,
  grocery and bank receipts, wine
  labels
• old dress patterns, tissue paper
• bronze leaf (optional)
• general craft supplies

TIPS
Use blank ready-cut postcards or try a sheet of 1-ply chipboard or cover stock for a large collage that can be cut into postcard-size pieces. Photocopy original materials and use the copies for the project.

ARTIST: IRENE KORONAS

These delicate ornaments recall the cutwork paper balls that children have made for ages; but the use of vellum paper adds to the translucent, contemporary design. Make these ornaments in all sizes and hang in groups or singly in each window. Add them to holiday centerpiece arrangements, or give them as gifts or package decorations. Experiment with embossing powders, stamps, and decorative paper punches to make each ornament unique.

vellum circle ornament

Makes one ornament

1 Using a plastic lid as a template, sketch twenty circles on vellum and cut them out with a craft knife. Cut a circle the same size from a piece of scrap cardboard. Using a protractor, draft an equilateral triangle with corners touching the edges of the circle; cut out to use as a template. Lightly mark the triangle on the wrong side of each circle and score the edges; turn the circles up in three sections along the scored edges.

2 Embellish each circle inside the scored triangle with rubber stamps, embossing powder, and cutwork as desired. Decorate circle edges with embossing powder or glitter.

3 Fold in scored flaps toward center on each circle. With a low temperature glue gun, attach five circles together by gluing the backs of the flaps together on two sides, triangle points to the center, completing the ball top by gluing the first circle to the fifth. Glue an additional circle to the bottom flaps of each of the original five circles, creating half a sphere. Set aside and repeat for the remaining ten circles. Glue the two ten-circle clusters together at open flaps to create the finished sphere.

4 Use a decorative paper edger to trim glued flaps if desired. Thread sheer ribbon through the ornament, adding beads, bells, or charms to the bottom, and tie off to finish.

VARIATION
Make a ball with large open cutwork inside the triangle sections and suspend a glass ornament inside.
Use decorative paper such as gift wrap, origami foils, or recycled greeting cards for colorful ornaments.

MATERIALS
- two sheets vellum
- plastic lid
- rubber stamps
- embossing powder
- decorative paper punches and paper edgers
- glue gun and glue
- sheer ribbon
- charms, beads, or bells
- protractor
- general craft supplies

TIPS
To make the spiral sections of the triangle faces, stamp a spiral design, emboss it with clear powder, then cut out the unembossed sections of the spiral with a craft knife. Use a circle cutter to facilitate cutting the circles from the vellum.

ARTIST: CINDY GORDER

Make collages from your keepsakes to create personal bookmarks that just might distract you from your reading. Fun for children to make as gifts for relatives or teachers, these page markers can be simple or complex, dainty or bold. Experiment with your collage arrangements before gluing objects to the paper, and consider adding printed papers and images to your final design.

keepsake bookmarks

Makes one bookmark

1 Trim handmade paper and card stock to desired bookmark size. Over a protected surface, apply spray adhesive to the wrong side of handmade paper. Place paper on cardstock and press firmly to bond papers together, smoothing out any air bubbles.

2 Stamp with rubber stamps and inks (optional).

3 Attach collage objects in a pleasing arrangement to handmade-paper side of bookmark with a glue gun.

4 Punch a hole at the top of the bookmark and add a ribbon loop or tassel as desired.

MATERIALS

- handmade paper
- card stock
- spray adhesive
- rubber stamps and ink (optional)
- found objects: pressed flowers and leaves, stamps, feathers, charms, buttons, lace, paper doilies
- glue gun and glue
- ribbon or tassels as desired
- general craft supplies

TIPS

Most spray adhesives bond quickly, so work fast when bonding the handmade paper to card stock. If you're making a number of bookmarks, glue the full-size sheet of handmade paper to the full-size sheet of card stock and cut multiple bookmark strips from the attached layers.

ARTIST: JUDY GRAVETT-PLAYER

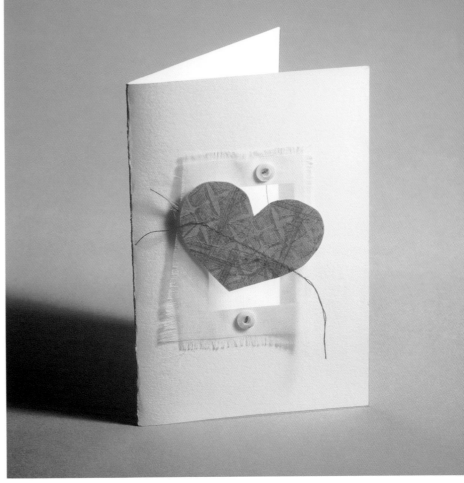

Add folk-art whimsy to your personal correspondence with this quick-to-create card. The sheer silk organza in this collage adds a layer of depth, while the button accents create elegant simplicity. In addition to cutting hearts from decorative paper, make other interesting cards using images cut from wrapping paper or magazines. Or, sew the organza to the inside window, and rubber-stamp a pattern around the window opening.

ARTIST: LISA KERR

organza window cards

Makes one card

1 Trim card stock to height and twice width of desired card and fold in half, or use purchased blank card. With a craft knife, cutting mat, and triangle, cut a centered 1 1/2" x 2" (4 cm x 5 cm) rectangle through the front face of the card.

2 Rough-cut a piece of silk organza larger than the window opening. Pull warp and weft threads to lightly fray edges on all sides. Cut a heart shape from the decorative paper and stitch to the center of the organza with a single straight machine stitch. Trim stitching threads to desired length.

3 Hand-sew the buttons to the top and bottom of the card opening to hold the organza over the face of the window.

VARIATION
Line the message area of the inside of the card with colored or decorative paper, which will show through the sheer organza scrim when closed.

MATERIALS

- card stock or purchased blank card
- silk organza
- decorative paper
- 2 buttons
- sewing machine
- general craft supplies

Photocopied acetate accents add a three-dimensional aspect to these playful greeting cards. Attached with brass fasteners, the transparent film tops a layered-paper card base. Look for strong black-and-white images from copyright-free art books, or sketch an original design to photocopy. Your choice of decorative papers and a handwritten word or phrase on the front of the card define the style.

acetate-accented
greeting cards

Makes one card

1 Photocopy selected images onto transparent film or acetate. Cut to desired size.

2 Cut card stock to height and twice width of desired card and fold in half, or use purchased blank card. Cut or tear a piece of decorative paper and glue to card face with PVA glue. Glue a piece of decorative paper to the inside of the card for a writing surface.

3 Place the acetate piece in position at the front of the card. Cut a small straight slit through the layers of the card face where you will insert the brass fastener. Slide the brass fastener through the slit, and spread the arms open on the back of the card face to secure the image. Repeat as desired.

4 Add handwritten messages to the card face with colored pens or metallic markers.

VARIATION
Instead of using a brass fastener to attach the acetate image, use photo corners or a single machine stitch, or cut four small diagonal slits and insert acetate edges in the openings to hold in place.

MATERIALS
• transparent copy film or acetate
• copyright-free art
• card stock or blank card
• decorative accent paper
• brass fasteners
• PVA glue
• general craft supplies

TIP
Most copy shops carry transparent film appropriate for use in copy machines, but you can also purchase the acetate sheets at office and art supply stores. Plan to fill the sheet's surface with designs to create multiple cards.

ARTIST: LISA KERR

These lightweight papier-mâché flowers add garden atmosphere to decorating projects. Whether used to adorn curtain ties or gift packages, they make excellent home accents or bridal shower favors. Paint the flowers to coordinate with window treatments or a party's color theme. Use the flowers to accent candles and table settings, too, or mount them on wire stems for an eclectic arrangement. Flowers may be covered with acrylic varnish for added durability.

sculpted flowers

Makes approximately six flowers

1 On printmaking paper, use pencil to draw a simple flower shape approximately 2" (5 cm) in diameter, leaving 3/4" (2 cm) diameter circle in center of flower. Cut the shape out with scissors and gently bend petals into a natural shape.

2 In a plastic bag, combine a small amount of papier-mâché mix with a small quantity of warm water according to manufacturer's directions. Seal the bag and knead until the contents are the consistency of bread dough, adding more water if necessary.

3 Moisten fingers with water, remove a pinch of papier-mâché dough from the bag, and roll it into a ball about the size of a large pea. Using your fingers or the end of a paintbrush handle, press the papier-mâché ball into the center of the paper flower. Let dry completely.

4 Paint the flower with acrylic paint, adding details with a fine brush. Repeat for remaining flowers. Let dry.

5 Attach the finished flowers to curtain tieback hardware with epoxy.

VARIATION

After the papier-mâché center is dry, create a double flower by attaching a second set of petals to the back of the flower with acrylic gel medium. Attach a pin back to the flower for a lovely summer brooch. To decorate gifts, attach the finished flowers to gift packages with white craft glue.

MATERIALS

- white 100% rag printmaking paper
- papier-mâché mix
- resealable plastic bag
- acrylic paint
- epoxy
- general craft supplies

TIPS

Draw the flower shape on cardboard to make a template that can be reused. The flower can be placed on a cookie sheet and put in a 140°F (60°C) oven for approximately 40 minutes to speed up the drying process of the papier-mâché center. Check at 20 minutes to see that it does not burn. Unused papier-mâché dough may be stored in the refrigerator for up to 3 days.

ARTIST: SARA BURR

The unique beauty of a combed paste-paper design is the perfect cover for this layered, pamphlet-stitched card. Write a special message on each page to personalize the greeting, or give the card blank for use as a mini-journal or sketchbook. Combine layers of decorative paper inside to customize the color scheme, or use blank writing paper and rubber-stamped interior accents. The simple pamphlet stitch holds the card together with a sophisticated touch.

pamphlet-stitched card

Makes one card

1 Cut one piece of paste paper, one piece of transparent paper, and two sheets of writing paper to height and twice width of desired card. Fold all sheets in half, and insert the writing paper inside the transparent paper, matching fold lines; then insert the group into the paste paper, again matching fold lines.

2 Measure and lightly mark three evenly spaced spots on the inner fold line for stitching. Holding card halfway open with the top layers together, pierce a small hole through all layers at the marks on the fold line with an awl or knitting needle.

3 Thread a length or cord or thin ribbon from the inside fold to the outside back through the top and bottom holes, using a sharp object to help force the cord through the holes if necessary. Bring each end from the outside back to the inside through the middle hole. Knot ends over the inside long stitch and trim.

VARIATION
Cut or tear the interior papers into decreasing sizes to create layers of pages.

MATERIALS
- paste paper (see page 13)
- writing paper or stationery
- transparent handmade paper embedded with petals
- cord or thin ribbon
- awl or knitting needle
- general craft supplies

TIP
Do not make the stitching holes at the fold too large or paper layers will be loose. If the ribbon is too wide to easily insert through the holes, fold it in half and use pliers to pull it through.

ARTIST: LISA KERR

The recipients of these artistic memento cards are likely to keep and frame them. Harmonize the cards with the season by utilizing colored leaves in the fall, summery beach glass and driftwood, or pressed pansies from the spring. Have a variety of scrap papers handy to compose the collages—look for different textures such as corrugated cardboard or handmade woven textures. And, pay special attention to the edges of the paper. Tear rough edges, carefully burn the sides, or age the border with tea or watered-down acrylic paint.

memento
greeting cards

Makes one card

1 Trim card stock to height and twice width of desired card and fold in half, or use purchased blank card.

2 Choose decorative papers for the collage and trim or tear to size. In a well-ventilated area, apply spray adhesive to the wrong side of paper over a protected work surface. Place on cardstock and press firmly.

3 Attach mementos in a pleasing arrangement to handmade paper with a glue gun.

MATERIALS

- card stock or purchased blank card
- decorative paper such as handmade or corrugated paper
- spray adhesive
- rubber stamps and ink (optional)
- found objects: feathers, driftwood, beach glass, shells, lace, pressed flowers and leaves, stamps, charms, buttons, paper doilies
- glue gun and glue
- general craft supplies

ARTIST: JUDY GRAVETT-PLAYER

TIP

If you don't have a convenient work area to use spray adhesive, use PVA glue to bond the papers together.

Fanciful and elegant collages are a unique way to distinguish a greeting card. Torn paper adds a rough and natural edge; insert a personal element to the mix such as old sheet music, fortunes from a Chinese restaurant, or pages from a long-loved book (photocopy these to keep the original intact). Use your sewing machine to create decorative patterns of stitching to hold the collage together—try a swirled pattern of stitching, experiment with a repetitive theme to add texture, or capture thread snippets and flower petals in the decorative stitching.

ARTIST: NANCY WORRELL

stitched
collage cards

Makes one card

1 Combine torn pieces of handmade paper, lace, and printed paper into a pleasing arrangement on sheer fabric. Sprinkle on flower petals, thread snippets, or ribbon as desired.

2 With a sewing machine, stitch the collage in a swirled or repetitive pattern that will secure all collage elements together.

3 Glue collage to card; let dry thoroughly.

MATERIALS

- blank greeting card and matching envelope
- handmade paper
- sheer fabric
- lace
- old sheet music
- flower petals
- thread snippets
- sewing thread
- PVA glue
- general craft supplies

The secret to making these surprising, textured cards is double-tack film, which easily adheres to paper and allows the placement and removal of a lace mask. Craft sand fills the unmasked area first, then the rest of the image is completed with another color of sand. When choosing an image, look for strong, recognizable silhouettes from large rubber stamps, old greeting cards, cookie cutters, and copyright-free art books.

silhouette
sand cards

Makes one card

1 Cut card stock to height and twice width of desired card and fold in half, or use purchased blank card. Sketch or find your desired image and transfer the shape onto double-tack adhesive film, enlarging or reducing size with a photocopier if necessary to fit. Cut out the shape from the film with scissors.

2 Peel off the paper backing from one side of the film, using a straight pin to separate edges if necessary. Adhere to the front of the card. Peel off the top paper covering from the film. Position the lace over the film, smoothing with your fingertips to secure.

3 Pour the first color of sand over the entire image. Brush away excess sand onto a creased piece of paper and pour extra back into container.

4 Remove lace from film. Sprinkle second color over image to fill in remaining areas of the image. Brush away excess sand and reserve for future use. Decorate the edges of the card with rubber stamps and ink if desired.

VARIATIONS

Substitute extra-fine glitter, granular spices such as salt or mustard, or poppy seeds for the sand. In addition to the lace, you can also add a nonpaper item such as a flat charm to mask off an area of the card for a third color of sand.

MATERIALS

- card stock or purchased blank card
- double-tack mounting film
- two colors of craft sand
- scrap lace pieces
- rubber stamps and ink
- general craft supplies

TIPS

Use empty film containers to hold sand for easy pouring. Mix sand colors together for variety. Choose contrasting colors of sand for greater detail.

ARTIST: LISA GLICKSMAN

This practical and pretty display provides handy storage for CDs, photos, or letters. Perfect for wedding or baby shower gifts, the boxes can be customized to any décor. This project uses plain or patterned grosgrain ribbon as a textural accent, as well as copper metallic rubbing compound for a distressed paint finish on the lid edges. Handwrite special words or phrases on the boxes to further personalize the set, and top it all off with a painted wooden medallion and bead.

embellished
papier-mâché boxes

Makes three boxes

1 Paint boxes and lids in desired base color of acrylic paint with a foam brush. Let dry. Paint the wood medallion and bead with the metallic copper acrylic paint and let dry.

2 Paint freehand designs on the sides of boxes using cream-colored acrylic paint with a round paint brush, using "comma" brush strokes for swirls and the brush end to make dots. Let dry.

3 Apply ribbon accents to the boxes using small amounts of thick white glue.

4 With your fingertips, apply copper metallic rubbing compound to the edges of the lids. Handwrite desired words on the edges with a metallic paint marker.

5 Glue the medallion and bead to the top of the small box. Seal entire project with matte acrylic spray sealer if desired.

VARIATION
Glue dried flower petals to the box sides and store seeds or other garden supplies.

MATERIALS
- three papier-mâché boxes
- wood medallion and round wooden bead
- craft acrylic paint in cream, mint, light sage, and metallic copper
- thick white glue
- 3 yards (2.7 m) 1" (2 cm) grosgrain ribbon
- copper metallic rubbing compound
- gold metallic paint marker
- matte acrylic spray sealer (optional)
- general craft supplies

TIP
Practice handwriting the words on a scrap piece of cardboard before writing on the box.

ARTIST: KELLY HENDERSON

Natural botanical prints of fresh leaves are showcased perfectly in a simple, monochromatic greeting card. Enjoy peaceful quiet time while foraging for the perfect leaf shapes and sizes to print. Store your leaves in a resealable bag, lay a moist paper towel in the bottom, and spray a fine water mist into the bag as needed to maintain moisture level. Refrigerate the bag if the leaves are not used immediately. Some leaves may stay fresh in this manner for many weeks.

botanical-print
cards

Makes one card

MATERIALS
- watercolor paper
- leaves
- crafter's ink
- brayer
- glue stick
- general craft supplies

1 To create the card, cut the watercolor paper into a long rectangle three times as long as it is tall. Fold the rectangle into three square sections of equal size, folding the left panel to the back of the center section, and folding the right panel to the front of the center section. Cut away a smaller square from the right panel, creating a frame for the center square when folded.

2 Pat dry a fresh leaf to remove any surface moisture. Apply crafter's ink to brayer. Over a protected work surface, gently roll ink onto leaf. Ink the entire surface area of the leaf, paying close attention to veins.

3 Carefully place leaf ink-side down onto center panel of card. Place a sheet of scrap paper over the leaf. Hold paper firmly in place and rub from the center of the leaf out to the tips with your hand or the back of a spoon. Rub over all surfaces of the leaf in this manner. Carefully lift scrap paper away from card, then remove leaf from card with tweezers. Let print dry.

4 Adhere the folded frame panel to the center panel with a dab of glue stick.

VARIATION
Experiment with other medium- to heavyweight papers for the card— each will give different results when the leaf image is transferred.

TIPS
If leaf surface is too irregular to use a brayer, use a dauber to apply the ink, or color the leaf surface directly with a marker. One leaf can be used to make many prints in the same or a different ink color. For your first efforts choose leaves that are more sturdy. Ink the front or the back of the leaf for different results.

ARTIST: MARTHA THURLOW

Complete your package-wrapping inventory with these unique gift cards. Tie them to ribbons and bows or attach them to jars and bottles of homemade treats. This decorative painting technique can be applied to many other paper projects, such as greeting cards, journal covers, hatboxes, or picture mats. For a rustic look, paint with natural tones, mount on corrugated cardboard, and use twine for the cord. Rubber stamp images on top to further personalize your tags.

paint-texturized
gift tags

ARTIST: MARY LAMB BECKER

Makes one gift tag

1 Mist the sheet of watercolor paper with water to pre-pare for painting. Dilute acrylic paint slightly with water and apply to paper with a foam brush, allowing paint to puddle in areas. Add an additional paint color in the same manner if desired. Immediately cover with a sheet of plastic wrap that is cut larger than the sheet of watercolor paper. Wrinkle the plastic wrap to texturize the wet paint. Let dry thoroughly.

2 Remove the plastic wrap. Cut the paper into gift tags approximately 2" x 3/4" (5 cm x 2 cm). Mount with PVA glue on card stock trimmed slightly larger than the watercolor sections.

3 Punch a centered hole on one end, and loop through ribbon or cord to finish.

VARIATION
Let paint dry completely, then add a very thick coat of acrylic medium before placing a large sheet of plastic wrap over paper. Manipulate plastic into folds and wrinkles. Leave wrap on and dry thoroughly, creating a glossy, textured finish. Trim as desired.

MATERIALS
- 1 sheet of watercolor paper
- spray water bottle
- acrylic paints
- plastic food wrap
- card stock
- PVA glue
- hole punch
- ribbon or gold cord
- general craft supplies

ARTIST: MARY LAMB BECKER

It's the details that matter at a dinner party. Your guests will love these dynamic place cards, which are accented with alternating strips of handmade paper cut on a diagonal. Use handmade papers in subtle tones for a harmonious accent to your table settings, or let the place cards take center stage with dramatic papers and ink. Use a calligraphy pen to write names for an elegant dinner, or for a charming touch, have your young children print the guest's names.

cut-paper place cards

Makes six place cards

1 Cut the decorative papers into one 1/2" x 8" (1 cm x 20 cm) strip each. Glue with long sides aligned onto a piece of card stock. Cut twelve 1/8" (.32 cm) wide strips diagonally across the paper.

2 Trim card stock into six 5 1/2" x 2 3/4" (14 cm x 7 cm) rectangles. Score each piece lengthwise, slightly off center so that the front face is taller than the back face. Fold cards on scoring line.

3 Adhere two diagonally striped strips to each place card in an X shape on the left side of card, extending upper ends of strips beyond fold line. Write name on card with a colored or metallic marker.

VARIATION
Use a rubber stamp and ink to create a border around the face of the place cards before gluing on paper strips.

MATERIALS
- five lightweight handmade or decorative papers
- card stock
- PVA glue
- metallic or colored pen
- general craft supplies

These handwoven baskets are actually recycled grocery bags. The printing from the bags lends an old-time graphic appeal to the final project. Paper grocery bags are surprisingly strong—the finished baskets are quite durable. This easy weaving technique can be adapted to create baskets of many sizes and shapes. Use them to hold paper clips and pens at your desk, or create a series of baskets in varying sizes for an eclectic display. Refer to diagrams A–D on page 162 while making this project.

woven
brown bag basket

Makes one basket

1 Cut off the bottom of one grocery bag at the folding line and discard the bottom section. Fold the top section in half, open end to open end; cut into two pieces along fold. Cut pieces open along seam line to create two strips that are approximately 6" x 36" (15 cm x 91 cm). Fold each strip in half lengthwise, then fold each long side in toward the center again, creating long strips of four layers. Repeat for remaining grocery bags.

2 Trim six paper strips to 28" (71 cm) lengths and place side by side. Weave four of the remaining 36" (91 cm) strips into the six shorter strips in an over-and-under pattern, leaving at least 6" (15 cm) edges on all sides (see diagram A). Fold up edge strips perpendicular to the woven base, and clip vertically in pairs with clothespins (see diagram B).

3 Beginning in the middle of one side, weave one paper strip around perimeter using an over-and-under pattern. (see diagram C). Repeat for two more strips, starting each row on a different side of the basket. Tighten the basket until no open spaces are visible between strips. Glue strip ends in place. Crease the corners and edges. Trim the top edge evenly. Put a drop of glue on the top horizontal strip at each vertical strip and clip with clothespins. Allow to dry; remove clothespins.

4 Fold the remaining paper strip over the top edge of the basket to finish (see diagram D). Clip in place with clothespins and crease corners. Blanket-stitch twine around the top strip to secure in place, sewing between intersections of the weave.

VARIATION
Use decorative paper to create small baskets for party favors and candy.

ARTIST: GAIL HERCHER

TIPS
Work with even numbers of strips and plan basket size in advance. The larger the basket, the wider, longer, and stronger the strips should be.

Black and white photographs have been hand-tinted to add color since the beginning of photography. Create instant heirlooms by adding romantic colors to photos using SpotPen's Handcoloring Pens. These special pens are a convenient and neat way to make vintage tinted images and are specially formulated to penetrate the photo emulsion so that they can be used on matte or glossy finishes. Use a light application of colors for aged and subtle images, or intensify the coloration for modern, quirky looks.

hand-tinted
photographs

1 Tape the photograph to the work surface to prevent curling. In a disposable container, mix 2 cups water and 1/2 teaspoon Photo-Flo. Solution can be stored if covered.

2 Lightly moisten a sponge in the solution. Press the damp sponge two or three times against first area to be tinted until the photo-emulsion becomes tacky. Blot any excess solution with a paper towel or cotton ball.

3 With a light circular motion, rub presoftened pen over treated area to release color. Color intensity builds with application, but heavy pressure may scratch the emulsion. Colors may be layered; work with light tones first.

4 Repeat steps 2 and 3 to tint each area as desired. Even out excess dye by blotting with a moistened paper towel. The dye remover pen (which should also be presoftened) will correct minor mistakes, tone down colors, and soften or blend colors at the edges as long as the initial application of dye has not dried. Let dry 2 to 4 hours.

VARIATION
Color only one area of the photograph, such as a face, a flower, or an architectural detail, for a special effect.

MATERIALS
- black and white photographs
- SpotPen Handcoloring pens
- SpotPen Dye Remover pen
- Photo-Flo premoistening solution
- general craft supplies

Wire Photo Stand
This versatile photo stand can be created in minutes with wire and pliers. Refer to the diagram on page 171 for parts A–C.

MATERIALS
- **16 gauge black annealed wire**
- **needle-nose pliers**
- **diagram (page 171)**
- **5/8" dowel or magic marker**

Makes one photo stand

1 Wrap wire at one end two times around dowel or magic marker. With pliers, bend the long end of wire 90° from wire circles to create a stem. Wrap the short end of wire around the stem just below the coils and trim (A).

2 Shape the wire stem into a triangular shape similar to a coat hanger, wrapping end around stem where it re-joins at midpoint of stand (B). Extend the end to the back of the stand, creating an easel back. Coil the end with pliers and trim to finish (C).

TIPS
Presoften the pen tips following manufacturer's instructions before their first use or the pens may scratch the photo emulsion. If new images are printed specifically for tinting, ask for them to be developed 10 percent lighter than normal for a background more receptive to the addition of color. Prints made on resin-coated paper will retain their form better. Fiber-based paper may curl when colored, requiring dry-mount pressing after completion. Read the manufacturer's inserts for more information on choosing a developing paper.

Like a patchwork quilt, this collage place mat combines colors and patterns to make a lively addition to the dining table. Exact placement of each square is not necessary, as the loose arrangement adds a clever, informal appearance to the place mat. Choose stamps in varying colors for the center accents, or cut images from magazines, gift cards, or wrapping paper to personalize. Customize a set of place mats to match the dining room décor or individualize them for a wedding or anniversary gift.

paper collage
place mat

Makes one place mat

1 Cut six 4" x 4" (10 cm x 10 cm) squares from each of the two background paper choices. Cut six 2" x 2" (5 cm x 5 cm) squares from each of the two foreground paper selections.

2 Brush decoupage medium on the backs of the larger squares and apply them to the canvas paper in an alternating pattern. Repeat to apply the smaller squares on the large squares. Glue the small images to the middle of each small square.

3 Sandwich the place mat between sheets of wax paper and place between heavy books overnight to dry flat.

4 Coat the place mat with 3–4 applications of decoupage medium, front and back, allowing to dry 20 minutes between coats.

VARIATION

Make coordinating coasters from single collage squares and 4" x 4" (10 cm x 10 cm) pieces of canvas paper.

MATERIALS

- 12" x 16" (30 cm x 41 cm) sheet of canvas paper
- two 8 1/2" x 11" sheets each of two background papers
- one 8 1/2" x 11" sheet each of two foreground papers
- 12 postage stamps or other small images
- decoupage medium
- general craft supplies

TIP

Make 4" x 4" (10 cm x 10 cm) and 2" x 2" (5 cm x 5 cm) squares from scrap cardboard to use as a template when cutting paper. Although the layers of decoupage medium will seal and protect the place mat against spills, use caution when cleaning. Wipe gently with a damp cloth or paper towel and do not submerge in water.

ARTIST: ANN KEGEL BAUSMAN

Gocco printing is a simple silk screening process that facilitates making multiple prints of the same design. Whether you choose to print directly on the card or onto cut pieces of paper to create a collage on the final project, this technique is a quick and easy way to create similar sets of note cards. Use them for thank-you notes or holiday greeting cards. Or, create a gift set of note cards and cover them with tea-dyed wrapping paper (see page 56).

gocco-print note cards

Makes one card

1 Cut card stock to height and twice width of desired card and fold in half, or use purchased blank deckle edged card. Cut another piece of card stock smaller than the card face for the printed image, or choose to print directly on the card.

2 Sketch an image on paper, or photocopy a copyright-free clip art selection. Following the manufacturer's directions, expose the drawing onto a sensitized screen in the Gocco machine with flash bulbs.

3 Lift the acetate top from the screen. Squeeze desired ink onto the design on the screen before lowering the acetate back into place. As directed, insert the screen into the top portion of the Gocco machine and line up the card stock underneath. Press the top of the Gocco machine to the card firmly. Remove card and let dry.

4 Cut collage accents from paper, trimming edges with decorative patterns as desired. Assemble collage to card face with PVA glue. Let dry.

VARIATIONS

Buy a rubber stamp with an appropriate phrase to stamp a message on the inside of the card. Use the Gocco silk screen process on fabric and machine-sew the print to a card.

MATERIALS
- card stock or blank deckle edged card
- Gocco machine
- Gocco paper inks
- decorative accent paper
- PVA glue
- general craft supplies

TIPS
Each screen will produce approximately fifty prints. See manufacturer's package insert for storage recommendations.

ARTIST: LISA KERR

Protect your tables with wild and primitive coasters that are deceptively simple to make—all you do is wrap cardboard with paper. Many papers will work well with this technique, so experiment with handmade and decorative sheets to match different rooms of the house or to change your seasonal decor. These creative coasters are very easy for children to make and give as presents—have them sign and date the bottom before varnishing, then tie the finished coasters together with raffia to create a set.

zebra-print coasters

Makes eight coasters

1 Cut chipboard into eight 4" (10 cm) circles.

2 Crumple the wrapping paper to distress. Cut eight 4 1/2" (11 cm) circles from the paper. Glue a chipboard circle to the center of the wrong side of each paper circle. Cut V-notches in the excess paper edge and glue to the underside of the chipboard.

3 Cut eight 4" (10 cm) circles from the wrapping paper and glue to the bottom of the covered chipboard, hiding the turned-over edges.

4 Seal the coasters with several coats of satin varnish applied with a foam brush, allowing to dry thoroughly between coats.

VARIATION
Glue a felt or cork circle on the bottom for additional tabletop protection.

MATERIALS
- 16" x 16" (41 cm x 41 cm) sheet 2-ply chipboard
- one sheet wrapping paper
- white craft glue
- water-based satin varnish
- general craft supplies

ARTIST: SARAH STALIE

TIP
Use the base of a glass or a lid as a guide for cutting circles.

These cards with inserted decorative book-marks are a perfect way to send a card and gift at the same time. Or, package them with special books for a coordinated present for a teacher, new retiree, or bookworm. This is a perfect project for children to make and give; have them try other bookmark shapes such as hearts, flowers, and diamonds. In addition to decorating the shapes with metallic markers, experiment with layered colored papers, decorative painting techniques, or glued cutouts from magazines.

ARTIST: LISA KERR

bookmark
gift cards

Makes one card

1 Trim card stock to height and twice width of desired card and fold in half, or use purchased blank card.

2 Cut three strips of 1/2" x 4" (1 cm x 10 cm) colored paper for the stems. Cut three star shapes from decorative paper. Embellish stars as desired with metallic and colored pens. Glue star shapes to stem pieces.

3 Open card flat and cut two 1" (3 cm) slits 1/2" (1 cm) apart with craft knife and cutting mat. Insert bookmarks through opening.

4 Cut a strip of paper to decorate insertion band, embellish as desired, and glue to band.

MATERIALS

- card stock
- decorative paper
- metallic and colored pens
- PVA glue
- general craft supplies

TIP
When attaching the decorative strip to the insertion band, make sure that the bookmarks remain removable.

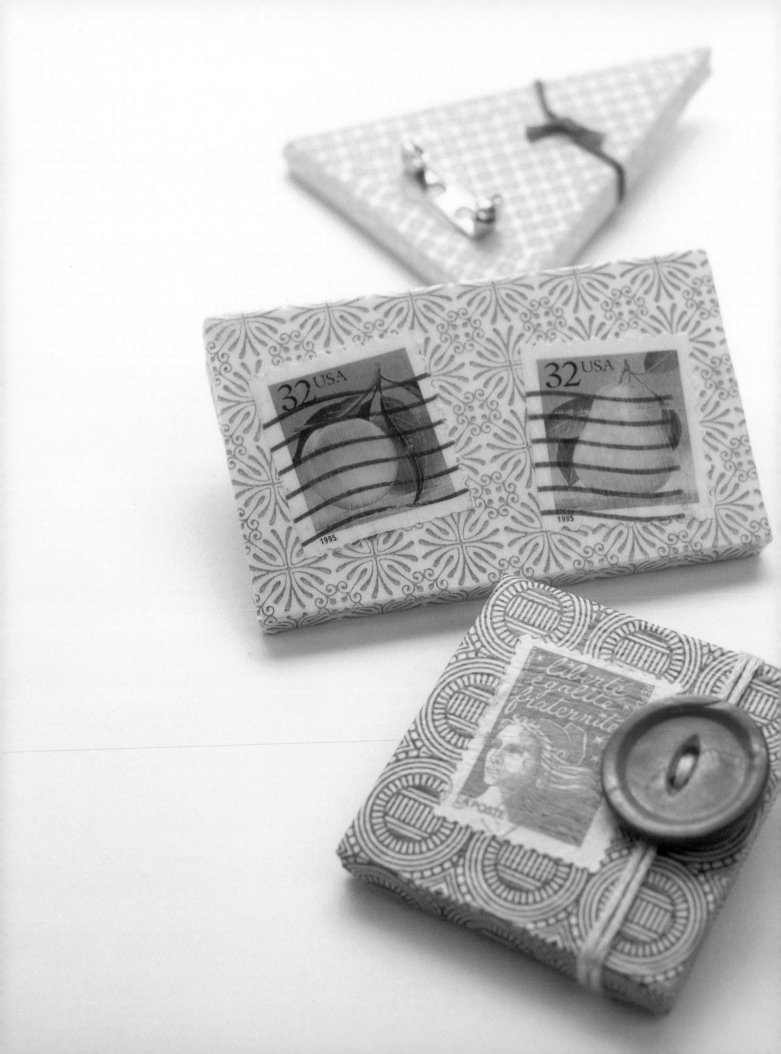

These fun and unique pins are easy to make for crafters of all ages. Create and wear a cluster of varying shapes such as square, triangles, and stars to add a playful touch to your wardrobe. Your choice of handmade paper, origami paper, or wrapping paper personalizes the jewelry. In addition to applying postage stamps to the pins, search for images or words from magazines and greeting cards, or substitute charms and other found treasures for the button.

paper collage pins

Makes one pin

1 Cut your desired pin shape from the foam core with a craft knife and cutting mat. Place the piece on the decorative paper and, with a pencil, trace an area 1/2" (1 cm) larger than the foam core shape. Cut the traced shape from the paper.

2 With a small brush, apply decoupage medium to one side of the foam core shape. Center the paper cutout, right side up, over the foam core and press to adhere. Apply decoupage medium to the overhanging edges of the paper and fold them to the back of the foam core as if wrapping a package, keeping edges neat and sharp. Adhere a postage stamp with decoupage medium to the front of the wrapped foam core, and allow to dry.

3 With a foam brush, coat the entire pin with several layers of decoupage medium to protect and seal the piece, waiting 15–20 minutes between coats. Let dry completely.

4 Thread embroidery floss through the button and wrap around the pin, knotting at the back. Add a drop of super glue to the back of the button and to the knot to secure. Glue pin back to the back of the piece with super glue, and let dry.

VARIATION
Instead of attaching a pin back, punch a hole at the top of the piece and insert a ribbon loop to make a pendant or ornament.

MATERIALS
• foam core
• decorative paper
• decoupage medium
• postage stamp
• button
• embroidery floss
• pin back
• super glue
• general craft supplies

TIP
Protect your work surface with waxed paper to prevent the pin from sticking while drying.

ARTIST: ANN KEGEL BAUSMAN

Custom window treatments have never been easier with this design, which incorporates natural papers, twigs, and twine. Leaves, flower petals, and the weave of the paper's fibers add subtle and elegant accents as the outdoor light shines through the handmade paper. The river-cane frame adds an informal yet stylish finish. In just one afternoon create shades for all your windows to add privacy and atmosphere, or piece together just one as a rustic wall hanging.

decorative paper
window shade

Makes one shade

1 Cut the four lengths of river cane to two inches longer than the width of the sheet of paper. With a hot glue gun, glue one piece of cane to the front top of the paper, then glue a second piece of cane to the back top of the paper, catching the paper between the canes. Repeat on the bottom edge of the paper with the remaining two pieces of cane.

2 Tie abaca twine to each side of the top cane lengths to form the hanger. Wrap the canes together on all four corners of the paper with several turns of twine, and finish with knots at the back.

VARIATION
Use sheer fabric instead of the paper, or substitute a painted dowel for the river cane and add stenciled or stamped accents.

MATERIALS
- four lengths of river cane
- one sheet handmade paper embedded with botanicals
- abaca twine
- glue gun and glue
- general craft supplies

TIPS
The size of canes and paper will vary depending on window size. Since the paper and cane pieces are not heavy, only a light bead of hot glue is necessary.

ARTIST: SANDI REINKE

This dramatic and sophisticated paper vase is perfect to hold a dry or silk floral arrangement or to display on its own. Layered papers create a harmonious collage that can coordinate or contrast with your décor. Choose papers that are semitransparent for creative color effects, or try patterned papers or magazine cutouts for a themed accent. Add an arrangement of sculpted paper flowers (see page 22) for a handmade housewarming gift.

layered-paper vase

Makes one vase

1 Spray the inside of the paper vase with metallic gold spray paint to seal.

2 Tear the handmade papers into 1" to 3" (3 cm to 8 cm) pieces. Beginning at the bottom of the vase, apply the paper pieces in a collage pattern with white craft or PVA glue, allowing the paper to wrinkle or fold as desired. Continue until entire vase is covered. Let dry 24 hours.

3 Apply two coats of acrylic gloss medium to seal vase surface, letting dry 2 hours between applications.

VARIATIONS
Embellish the papers with paints and markers before tearing into pieces, or use tissue papers for translucent color effects.

MATERIALS
• paper vase form
• metallic gold spray acrylic
• assorted decorative handmade papers
• white craft or PVA glue
• acrylic gloss medium
• general craft supplies

TIPS
Use a scrap cotton cloth such as a piece of T-shirt to press the torn pieces of paper to the vase after application to ensure that the paper edges are glued down.

ARTIST: KATHY CARTIER

This charming and elegant sconce shade made from parchment paper and a copyright-free antique ironwork design will add a vintage European look to your home décor. Applying styrene to the parchment before attaching it to a purchased wire lampshade frame adds durability to the final piece. Line a hallway with multiple shades for an architectural lighting effect, create just one for accent lighting, or, use as a nightlight for a dark corner of your home.

image-transfer
sconce shade

Makes one lampshade

1 Enlarge template from page 163 and photocopy onto parchment paper for a finished size of approximately 3 1/2" x 9 1/2" (9 cm x 24 cm). Lightly spray with sealer to prevent toner from smudging. Let dry. Cut out pattern, leaving a margin of 1" (3 cm) on all sides.

2 Cut a piece of styrene to the same size as the parchment. Peel the backing from the styrene, exposing the adhesive back. Place the parchment right side up onto the styrene and press to adhere. Hold the paper to the wire form so that the design is centered and trim shade to 3/8" (1 cm) beyond wire on all sides.

3 Brush a scant 3/8" (1 cm) line of glue on the front of one edge of the shade and apply ribbon. Repeat for remaining edges, mitering corners. Let dry for one hour.

4 Lay shade facedown and apply a generous bead of glue 3/8" (1 cm) from all sides. Set edge of frame on glue line at one short end of the shade and secure with clothespins, cushioning pins with scrap cardboard. Roll the frame along the glue lines to the other short edge, and secure as before with clothespins. Let dry overnight.

VARIATION
Search clip-art books for other ironwork designs.

MATERIALS
- 4 3/4" x 4 1/4" (12 cm x 11 cm) wire lampshade frame to fit candelabra bulb
- 8 1/2" x 14" (22 cm x 36 cm) parchment paper
- template (see page 163)
- self-adhesive styrene
- 1 yard (.9 m) 3/8" (1 cm) wide black grosgrain ribbon
- Mainly Shades quick-dry glue
- spray sealer
- spring-clip clothespins
- general craft supplies

TIP
To ensure safety, only use with bulbs of 40 watts or less.

ARTIST: DAWN ANDERSON

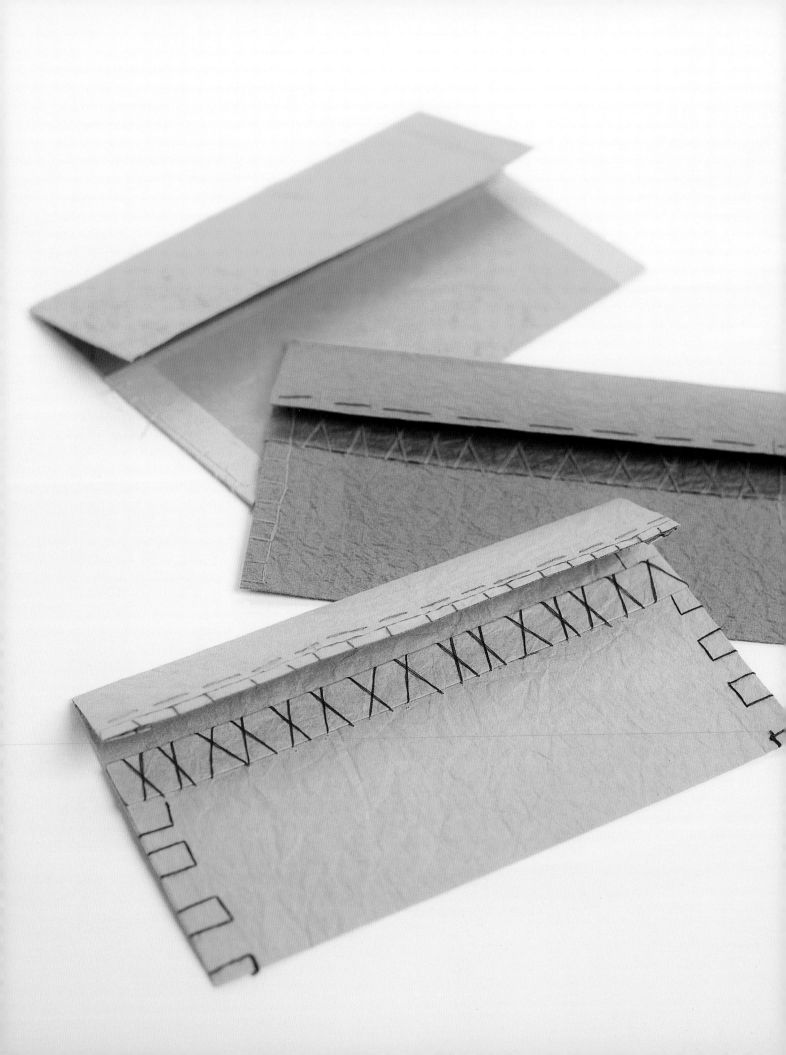

Once you've made any of the greeting card projects in this book, create a complementary envelope to complete the package. Hand stitching in colorful threads accents these decorative paper envelopes. Vary the weight and texture of the decorative paper to coordinate with the enclosed card, and use embroidery thread or multiple strands of sewing thread to add contrast and texture. Experiment with cross-stitch, blanket-stitch, and straight-stitch patterns to customize each envelope.

hand-stitched
paper envelope

Makes one envelope

1 Cut a rectangle from the decorative paper three times longer and 2" (5 cm) wider than the card you wish to enclose. Fold rectangle in thirds along the long edge. Fold the edge of the bottom third forward 1" (3 cm) and sew in place with a decorative cross stitch.

2 Fold long edges 1/2" (1 cm) to the inside. Fold back finished bottom section in place and blanket-stitch sides to seal.

3 Trim top third section to desired size plus 1/2" (1 cm) to make closing envelope flap. Fold edge 1/2" (1 cm) to the front and sew flat with a straight or decorative hand stitch.

VARIATIONS

Apply contrasting strips of paper to edges or center panel with PVA glue for more colorful envelopes. Make multiple folds on edges and combine decorative stitches for more complex designs.

MATERIALS
- decorative paper
- contrasting threads
- general craft supplies

TIPS
Vary the measurements for these envelopes to make seams and folds wider or smaller as desired. Test the envelope size periodically by inserting the card to ensure fit.

ARTIST: LISA KERR

For a beautiful gift or guestroom accent, wrap handmade soap in torn, tea-stained paper and ribbon and seal with wax for a finishing touch. Dying with tea is an inexpensive way to tint or age paper. Any kind of tea can be used—herbal, black, or green—with varying results. This multilayered wrapping effect is also perfect for presenting groups of candles, coaster sets, and small journals or books.

tea-dyed paper wrapping

Makes one package

1 Tape the bars of soap together to secure. Tear the watercolor paper into a strip approximately 3" (8 cm) wide and long enough to wrap around the soaps with an overlap at the ends. Tear the handmade paper into a strip 2" (5 cm) wide and the same length as the watercolor paper.

2 Steep tea bags in hot water for 20 minutes. Soak paper strips in room-temperature tea until they have reached the desired color. Paper will dry to a darker shade. Attach the paper to a clothes hanger at top edge with clothespins to dry. Let dry completely.

3 Wrap the watercolor paper around the soap and secure in place with glue gun or double-sided tape. Adhere pressed rose leaves to paper. Center the handmade paper strip on top of the watercolor paper; wrap around soap and secure with glue gun or double-sided tape.

4 Tie a ribbon around the soap and trim ends. Emboss seal at the tie with sealing wax and ring.

VARIATIONS

Instead of soaking the paper in the tea, spritz tea onto paper with a spray bottle for a mottled effect. Rubber-stamp the paper for more customized designs, or recycle antique papers such as old sheet music or damaged poetry books.

MATERIALS

- two bars of soap
- one piece of watercolor paper
- one piece of handmade paper
- one family-size teabag or three regular tea bags
- clothespins and hanger
- glue gun and glue or double-sided tape
- pressed rose leaves
- 18" (46 cm) ribbon
- sealing wax and ring
- general craft supplies

TIP

First tea-stain a scrap of paper to test for the paper's ability to withstand moisture and to determine dying time needed to achieve the desired tint.

ARTIST: KELLEY TAYLOR

fabric projects

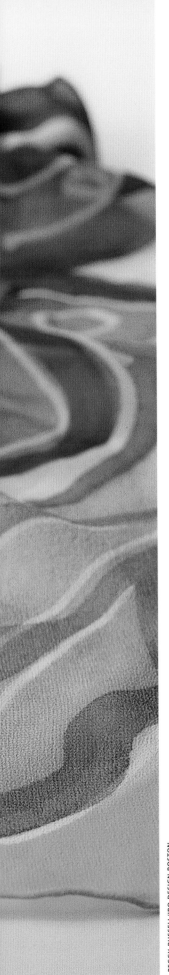

ARTIST: PEGGY RUSSELL/IRO DESIGN BOSTON

The vibrant colors of a hand-painted silk scarf of your own design can make an outfit sing. Let the color palette determine the mood of the scarf; try designing a few in the same pattern with different color selections to coordinate with the season. Take inspiration by any image you see—from simple color-blocked designs to botanical prints. With this simple technique, you paint directly from squeeze bottles filled with dye for creative control.

hand-painted silk chiffon scarf

Makes one scarf

1 Prewash your scarf according to manufacturer's recommendations to remove any sizing. Stretch a piece of canvas or heavy fabric on your table surface to use as a drop cloth. Pin the scarf around its perimeter to the drop cloth with ball headed pins, stretching the scarf as taut as possible. Place the pins on the hem of the scarf to prevent tearing holes in the material.

2 Begin by sketching your design lightly in pencil on the scarf. Fill in the first color by painting directly with a squeeze bottle filled with procion silk dye and a fixing agent, thickened with sodium alginate, following the manufacturer's directions. Trace the outside of the dye with a stiff, acrylic-quality paintbrush to create a sharper edge if desired. Allow to dry to the touch.

3 Apply resist paste to the areas that will remain white. Allow to dry.

4 Apply the other colors of procion dye in remaining white areas using a 1" (3 cm) wide foam brush or squeeze bottles. Allow to dry thoroughly between colors. When design is complete, follow the dye manufacturer's directions to set for steam setting. Rinse thoroughly. Towel dry and iron to finish.

VARIATIONS
Instead of the squeeze bottle technique, try sponging or stamping images, or cut a stencil form from coated cardboard or plastic. Use this technique also on yards of heavier-weight silk to create decorator fabrics for pillow shams and quilts. Or purchase solid silk tops and bottoms and embellish with your own designs.

MATERIALS
- white silk scarf
- canvas or cotton drop cloth
- procion silk dyes
- sodium alginate (seaweed crystals)
- fixing agent for dye
- resist paste
- plastic squeeze bottle applicator
- general craft supplies

TIPS
Layer the dye as you would watercolors to create shade, contour, and shadowing. Many brands of silk dyes are available, each requiring a different method to set the color. Look for a dye, such as the liquid procion used here, that can be heat-set without using expensive commercial equipment.

This comfortable and decorative pillow combines the rich deep colors of velvet with sophisticated embossed designs. A warm addition to your décor, these pillows are simple to sew but can be easily modified with piping, tassels, or fringe. Embellish one or both sides of the pillow with a repeating motif, and create a sofa-full in complementary colors, or add a bleached-velvet pillow (see page 84) to the mix for an eclectic decorating statement.

embossed
velvet pillow

Makes one pillow

1 Set iron to wool/cotton setting with steam off. On ironing board, place one square of velvet nap-side down over the patterned portion of the metal tool or stamp. Spray the back of the fabric with water until damp. Place iron over the stamp and hold stationary with even pressure for 15–20 seconds. To facilitate even design transfer, use the area of the iron that doesn't have steam holes if possible. Repeat as desired.

2 With right sides of velvet pieces facing, sew three sides of fabric together with a 1/2" (1 cm) seam allowance. Turn pillow right side out. Insert pillow form, and whip-stitch fourth side closed.

VARIATION
Add decorative piping to the pillow by sewing contrasting velvet around piping cord, then pinning the covered piping to the inside edges of the fabric before sewing, matching the seam of the piping to the seam allowance of the pillow. Sew the three sides of the pillow together, then tack the piping to the fourth side and sew in a zipper for easy removal of the pillow form when cleaning the velvet.

MATERIALS
- two 13" (33 cm) square pieces of velvet
- metal batiking tool, rubber stamp, or wood block
- iron and ironing board
- spray water bottle
- sewing machine
- 12" (30 cm) pillow form
- general craft supplies

TIP
Velvets made from different fibers yield varying results when embossed. Test emboss velvet scraps to check for iron pressing time. Any heat-resistant item can be used to emboss the fabric: Experiment with coiled wire, coat hangers, or metal cookie cutters to create the impression.

ARTIST: MARTHA THURLOW

The look of cut velvet is enhanced by beadwork on these fragrant sachets, which can be tucked into drawers but are pretty enough to leave out. Fusible webbing and rubber stamps are the key to creating sumptuous cut velvet with ease. Fill the sachets with lavender, or substitute scented potpourri, crushed rose petals, or even spices; embellish them with silk ribbon embroidery or decorate with special charms or buttons. Place these lovely sachets all over your home—in dressers, armoires, front halls, and linen closets.

cutwork velvet sachets

Makes one sachet

1 Stamp a design onto the paper side of the fusible webbing with acrylic paint. When dry, trim the web close to the edges of the stamped image. Following the manufacturer's directions, fuse the cutout shapes to the wrong side of the velvet.

2 Working from the wrong side of the fabric, cut the design out of the velvet with a sharp craft knife on a protected surface. Carefully remove the paper backing. Fuse the velvet cutwork to the sheer fabric with an iron according to the manufacturer's recommendations.

3 Trim to the desired shape and size for a sachet, leaving 1/4" (.5 cm) or more for seams. Cut a similarly sized backing piece from sheer fabric or velvet. With right sides facing, sew both pieces together to make a pouch, leaving an opening for turning and filling.

4 Turn right side out and embellish the front and edges with sewn-on beadwork, using a beading needle and thread. Fill the pouch with lavender buds, and whip stitch closed. Add ribbon loop for hanging if desired.

VARIATIONS

Trace stencil designs on the fusible web instead of using stamps. Substitute silk instead of sheer fabric as a base for the cut velvet (but use sheer fabric on the back to allow the lavender fragrance to escape).

MATERIALS
- velvet
- sheer fabric
- paper-backed fusible webbing
- rubber stamps
- acrylic paint, any color
- assorted beads
- beading thread and needle
- dried lavender buds
- ribbon
- general craft supplies

TIPS
Iron the velvet facedown on another piece of velvet to prevent crushing the nap. If parts of the stamp design are too small for easy cutting, modify them for simplicity.

ARTIST: CINDY GORDER

Dramatic and unique, these napkins are the perfect accessories for a bold table setting. Select a single color of fabric paint or combine tones to complement your dishes, place mats, and tableware. Create two sets of coordinating napkins for a personalized gift, or make color-themed sets for your own seasonal table décor. Rock salt pulls away the paint pigment, resulting in the mottled, shaded effect. Silk fabric paint has a thinner consistency than craft fabric paints, so it responds well to the salting technique.

salt-dyed napkins

Makes four napkins

1 Prewash and dry fabric to remove sizing. Cut into four 17" (43 cm) squares.

2 Mist fabric squares until thoroughly damp. Place on a sheet of freezer paper. With a foam brush, paint napkins with fabric dyes. Paint in large patterns; colors will seep slightly into each other. Sprinkle a handful of rock salt on each piece of fabric, randomly or in patterns. Let dry thoroughly. Remove salt and wash napkins in cold water. Dry and iron.

3 Pull warp and weft threads on napkin edges to fray. Machine-stitch 1/4" (.5 cm) from frayed edges.

VARIATIONS
Use the dyed fabric to create a coordinating table runner or pillows.
After fabric has dried, rubber stamp with acrylic fabric paint.

MATERIALS
- 1 yard (.9 m) 100% cotton muslin
- spray water bottle
- silk fabric paints
- freezer paper
- rock salt
- sewing machine
- general craft supplies

TIP
Dye all napkins in a set at the same time to ensure consistent results.

ARTIST: C. D. CARTWRIGHT

This handmade purse combines colors and textures of fabric to make a versatile wardrobe accessory well suited to both special occasions and casual shopping. The contrasting top fabric is folded partially inside the bag to meet the lining, creating a decorative finished appearance. You can adapt this project to make purses of any size, varying the colors and fabric finishes to coordinate with particular outfits or color schemes. Fill a handbag with travel-sized cosmetics for a personalized gift.

satin trim
handbag

Makes one handbag

1 Cut a rectangle from the velour fabric for the base section the desired width of the purse and two times the desired height of the section, plus 1/2" (1 cm) on each side for seam allowance. Snip two small notches on each short end, one inch in from the corner for future cord insertion. Cut a same-sized rectangle from the lining fabric. Trim two pieces of satin, each the same width of the short side of previous fabrics, and two times the height plus 1" (3 cm) of desired height of the top section of bag. Create two notches on one long edge of each top piece, each notch 1" (3 cm) from the corner, corresponding to notch placement on the base piece.

2 Sew a top piece at the un-notched long side to each short end of the lining fabric with a 1/2" (1 cm) seam allowance. Press seams flat. Trim two lengths of cord for straps. Baste straps at outside notches, with handles turned inside to center of right side of fabric, leaving at least 1/2" (1 cm) of cord overhanging edge.

3 Pin velour base section to short ends of top pieces, right sides together and matching notches. Stitch short ends with a 1/2" (1 cm) seam allowance, reinforcing areas around straps to ensure the handbag's durability. You will now have fabrics sewn in a complete circle, right sides and handles facing inside.

4 Pin fabric flat, folding in the middle of the brocade fabric on both ends, with lining and velour pieces matching at seams. Sew one side closed from top to bottom with a with a 1/2" (1 cm) seam allowance. Stitch the other side from the middle to one end, leaving an opening on one edge. Clip corners, and turn right side out at opening. Whip-stitch opening closed.

5 Fold the lining into the inside of the handbag and press.

VARIATIONS
Customize the fabric even further by using embossed or bleached velvet (see pages 62 and 84) or any of the many fabric treatments from the Crafter's Recipe Book.

MATERIALS
- velour for bag base
- satin brocade for top trim
- lining fabric
- cording
- sewing machine
- general craft supplies

TIP
This project can also be handsewn, if a sewing machine is not available.

ARTIST: LEE STRASBURGER

A woven pattern of thick and thin sheer ribbons creates a lovely dresser scarf. The varying sizes of the ribbon result in a simple plaid design from the over-and-under basket weaving. This project is a perfect accent for your dresser, vanity, or bedside tables, and also makes a wonderful gift. Choose colors that coordinate with your decorating scheme and place a special jewelry box or boudoir lamp on top.

woven-ribbon
dresser scarf

Makes one scarf

1 Determine the length and width of your desired dresser scarf. Cut ribbons to desired length plus 2" (5 cm). Lay ribbons side by side lengthwise and pin top edge to an ironing board, alternating colors and widths until you reach the desired width. These ribbons will be the warp of the weaving.

2 Cut additional ribbons to your desired width of the final project plus 2" (5 cm) to use for the weft of the weaving. Beginning 1" (3 cm) below the top of warp ribbons, weave the weft ribbons horizontally across the warp ribbons in an alternating over-and-under pattern, pinning each row immediately next to each other, and leaving a 1" (3 cm) overhang on each end. Alternate colors and widths of weft ribbons in a repeating pattern until you have woven your desired length. Apply strips of tape to the edges of the weaving to temporarily secure ribbons in place.

3 Machine-stitch a decorative or zigzag stitch along the outside ribbon to secure all ribbons in place. Remove tape and trim excess ribbon to desired length.

MATERIALS

- 1 1/2" (4 cm) and 7/8" (2 cm) wide sheer tan ribbons
- 1 1/2" (4 cm) and 5/8" (1.5 cm) wide sheer green ribbons
- 5/8" (1.5 cm) wide sheer gold ribbon
- sewing machine
- straight pins
- general craft supplies

ARTIST: ELAINE SCHMIDT

Makes one slipcase

1 Mix wheat paste with water to yogurt consistency, following package instructions. Let sit for 30 minutes, and strain out any lumps. Cut vintage fabric slightly larger than project requires so that grain (selvage) parallels the book's spine. Press fabric and lay facedown on work surface; mist lightly with water. Cut a piece of rice paper in the same grain direction, 1" (3 cm) larger on all sides than fabric.

2 Apply a thin coat of wheat paste to paper from the center out. Press a dowel against one edge of paper and lift. Hold paper by hand on edge opposite dowel, paste-side down, and carefully place on fabric from the middle out to the edges. Run a dry brush across the paper from the center out to remove air bubbles. Use a tightly rolled dishtowel to gently tamp paper from the center out, covering whole area. Lift carefully, and transfer to drying board, brushing the overhanging pasted paper edges smooth to the board. Let dry overnight. Remove from drying board by sliding a palette knife under edges to release.

3 Measure and cut the binder board with a mat knife according to the diagram on page 164, using the following measurements: two side pieces (height is height of your book plus 1/4" [.4 cm], width is width of book plus 1/8" [.3 cm]), two top and bottom wall pieces (height is depth of book, width equals width of book), and one spine wall piece (height equals depth of book, width is height of your book plus 1/4" [.5 cm]).

4 Apply PVA glue along long edge of the three wall pieces and along the short edges of the top and bottom wall pieces. Press onto one of the sidepieces, abutting each one at two corners.

5 With chisel and mallet, pound a slit into the remaining sidepiece, about 2" (5 cm) from the back edge. Thread the ribbon through the slit, allowing about 1" (3 cm) to hang through to outside face. Dig out an area of board so that ribbon can lay flush to surface; glue ribbon down. Glue the edges of this piece and place onto the assembled walls, with the long end of the ribbon dangling inside the completed box.

6 Cut the prepared fabric or book cloth to a height equaling the height of the box plus two times the depth of the box, and to a width equaling two times the width of the box plus the depth and 1 1/2" (4 cm). Place the cloth facedown on a papered work surface. Brush PVA glue onto back of cloth from the center out to edges. Working quickly, place the box onto the cloth, open side to the right, 3/4" (2 cm) from right side of paper and centered from top to bottom. Lift and roll box to the left, pressing it onto remaining cloth.

7 Finish the top and bottom ends as if wrapping a present, trimming away excess cloth. Turn in ends at opening, adding more glue if necessary. Place under a weight such as telephone books or a dictionary for 24 hours until completely dry.

MATERIALS
- vintage natural fabric
- acid-free rice paper
- 1/8" (.3 cm) thick binder board
- ribbon
- wheat starch paste (powder)
- PVA glue
- diagram (see page 164)

VARIATION

Make a second, smaller case to slip inside the first in the opposite direction to create a two-piece storage slipcase for photos or other keepsakes.

TIP

Use purchased book cloth if desired. To slow the drying time of PVA glue, cut with water, or mix one part wallpaper paste to one part glue. Glue acid-free paper to the binder board with the grain before cutting to create a lining for the slipcase.

ARTIST: LAUREL PARKER

Protect a special book with this stylish and useful slipcase that has been covered with vintage fabric recycled from a favorite vintage dress. The fabric is backed with acid-free rice paper to inhibit glue seepage and to stabilize its weave and prevent distortion. A ribbon is attached to the inside of the box to facilitate book removal. Create a slipcase for a treasured book, or use it to hold a journal, diary, or sketch book.

fabric
slipcase

A simple lampshade is transformed by transferring images from slide photographs to fabric using the Polaroid image transfer process. The special print film has an extended tonal range that enhances the dreamy, watercolor-like hues of the original photographs, making the final transfers glow in the lamplight. This sophisticated decorating technique is appropriate for any series of images, from landscape panoramas to architectural details. Imperfections in the transferred prints add interest to the final piece.

photo-transfer lampshade

ARTIST: MARGARET TIBERIO

Makes one lampshade

1 Expose your chosen slide in the slide printer onto the appropriate Polaroid instant print film specified by printer manufacturer. The film and printer types determine the size of the print. See package information for more details.

2 Rough-cut a piece of fabric large enough to hold selected print size. Soak in warm water and place damp fabric onto a glass pane or other smooth, hard surface. Excess water should be blotted from the fabric.

3 Pull the exposed film through the rollers of the slide printer. Wait ten seconds, then peel the image apart. Quickly place the negative carefully onto the fabric. With a brayer, roll across the image 4–6 times in one direction using medium pressure.

4 Keep negative in contact with fabric for two minutes while keeping both warm by running a hair dryer evenly over the surface, testing the back of the negative with your fingers to monitor heat level. After two minutes, remove negative carefully by peeling back diagonally from one edge.

5 Allow image to dry thoroughly. Trim the fabric to the image. Using a small amount of adhesive, apply the image to the outside of a plain fabric lampshade. Repeat for remaining sides.

VARIATIONS

Embellish the transferred image with fabric paints or dyes, or stain the final fabric print with tea to age. Use larger sheets of fabric decorated with transferred images to make pillows or place mats.

MATERIALS

• developed slide film
• instant slide printer
• Polaroid Type 669, 59, 559, or 809 film
• 100% silk or cotton fabric
• 8" x 10" (20 cm x 25 cm) glass pane
• brayer
• hairdryer
• white craft glue
• plain fabric lampshade
• general craft supplies

TIPS

Peeling the Polaroid negative apart sooner than ten seconds may result in a fogged image. Using heavy pressure to roll the negative with the brayer may distort the image; too little pressure creates white spots on the transfer. Do a few test pieces to acquaint yourself with the process.

A special gift for a mother-to-be, this quilt modernizes the tradition of a sewing bee. Color transfers, created easily at copy shops and reflecting the artistic efforts of a group of friends, are harmonized into one heirloom piece. Copyright-free art, also called "clip art," is a wonderful resource to find ironwork or other designs. Use the same three crayons in varying combinations for each square. Having a group of friends color the squares makes the whole greater than the sum of its parts.

photocopy-transfer
friendship quilt

Makes one quilt

1 Choose twelve ironwork squares from a clip art book, or sketch your own designs. Using a black-and-white photocopying machine, enlarge square to 2 3/4" (7 cm) on each side. Color each square with the same three crayons.

2 Take the completed squares to a copy shop that offers color transfers. Enlarge each design to a 6" (15 cm) square onto transfer paper. Trim each transfer so that there is no more than 1/4" (.25 cm) of white space surrounding each colored design

3 Create a template from grid paper measuring 10 1/2" (27 cm) square, and cut out a 6" (15 cm) square from the center. Cut out twelve 10 1/2" (27 cm) squares from the cotton fabric using the template as a guide. Cover a wood surface with a pillowcase. Place a fabric square face up on the surface, smoothing to remove wrinkles, and position one transfer facedown at the center using the grid-paper template to check placement. Remove the template and iron the transfer to the fabric with a dry iron, moving the iron from edge to edge in a circular motion for a count of thirty, or according to transfer manufacturer's directions. Remove the backing from the transfer by peeling back slowly from one edge. Repeat for remaining squares.

4 Pin completed squares together, three across and four down. Sew with a 1/4" (.5 cm) seam on all edges; press seams open. Cut a 30 1/2" x 40 1/2" (77 cm x 103 cm) section from both the cotton fabric and batting for a backing panel and filling. Pin the right sides of both the front and back fabrics to one another and place batting on top. Sew a 1/4" (.5 cm) seam through all layers around the edge, leaving a 12" (30 cm) opening at the bottom.

5 Turn the blanket right side out. Turn in the edges of the 12" (30 cm) hole and slip-stitch closed. Using white quilting thread and a large needle, tack the points where four corners meet by sewing a single stitch from the front of the quilt through the back of the quilt, then back to the front. Knot and trim thread to 1" (3 cm). Repeat for the remaining five cross sections.

MATERIALS

- copyright-free art
- 3 crayons
- black-and-white and color photocopying machines
- 11" x 17" (28 cm x 43 cm) pad of graph paper
- color copy iron-on transfer sheets
- 4 yards (3.7 m) smooth cotton fabric
- iron
- old pillow case
- quilt batting
- sewing machine
- white quilting thread
- large embroidery needle
- general craft supplies

TIPS

If your copy shop does not stock transfer paper, you can purchase the 8 1/2" x 11" (22 cm x 28 cm) sheets at an office supply store. Most color transfers are machine washable, but refer to the manufacturer's directions for specific washing instructions.

ARTIST: LAURA MCFADDEN

Make these unique napkins by using a stamp of your own design,
created by carving a printmaking block or eraser. From impres-
sionistic swirls to themed icons, the stamp's image is literally in
your hands. You can combine multiple stamps for an integrated
design as shown, or use a simple repeating pattern of one image.
Coordinate table linens by using the same color of ink on
contrasting fabrics, or apply this technique to purchased place
mats for a wonderful housewarming gift set.

hand-cut
stamp napkins

Makes four napkins

1 Design a simple image by either drawing directly on the printmaking block or eraser, or by sketching a design on paper and
transferring the final selection to the block. Note: Your design
will print as a mirror image of your stamp.

2 Holding the blade handle of a #1 linoleum cutter blade at a 45°
angle to the block, begin carving away the nonprinting areas of
the image with a gliding motion. Switch to a larger blade to
remove more block or eraser material. Only a 1/8" (.32 cm) layer
of the block needs to be removed to create a nonprinting
area. Proof the image periodically by tapping it in an inkpad
and stamping a scrap piece of paper until you are satisfied
with the results.

3 Prewash napkins to remove sizing. Dry according to
manufacturer's directions and press flat.

4 Plan the napkin's design by stamping a piece of paper cut to the
napkin's dimensions until you are pleased with the layout.
Stamp each napkin with the fabric ink according to the final
pattern. Let dry completely. Follow ink manufacturer's directions
to set the dye.

VARIATION

Try this stamping method on a canvas tote bag and use as a carry-all
for the beach.

MATERIALS

• soft printmaking block or eraser
• linoleum cutting tools
• ink pad
• fabric or crafting ink
• four napkins
• general craft supplies

TIPS

When carving the stamp, be
careful to not dig in too deeply
and gouge the material. Carve
from the center towards the sides
to avoid accidental cuts through
the middle of the design. Rotate
the block as you carve, position-
ing your fingers out of the blade's
path.

ARTIST: LILY MORRIS

Romantic and whimsical, these delicate creations from stitched thread are simple to make with a sewing machine and water-soluble fabric. The overlapping machine stitching holds the heart together like a fine crochet lace after the stabilizing fabric is dissolved. In addition to stitching in snippets of thread, capture bits of fabric and ribbon inside the heart, or whip-stitch around the edge with a narrow ribbon or decorative thread to finish. Explore other forms for these ornaments, such as stars, crescent moons, diamonds, and leaves.

thread-lace hearts

ARTIST: NANCY WORRELL

Makes one ornament

1 Cut two pieces of water-soluble embroidery fabric just bigger than the embroidery hoop. Use the disappearing ink marker to draw a heart motif in the center of the fabric.

2 Sandwich snippets of thread between the two pieces of fabric, inside the boundaries of the drawn heart. Place the fabric in the embroidery hoop.

3 Outline the heart three times using a medium-length zigzag stitch on the sewing machine. Fill in the heart design with a random mixture of connecting straight and zigzag stitches.

4 Remove the fabric from the hoop and trim the excess fabric to the edges of the stitched embroidery. Follow manufacturer's instructions for dissolving fabric. When ornament is dry, tie on a length of ribbon for hanging.

MATERIALS
- water-soluble embroidery fabric
- disappearing ink marker
- thread snippets
- embroidery hoop
- zigzag sewing machine
- ribbon
- general craft supplies

TIPS

Be sure the fabric is very tight in the embroidery hoop to make stitching easier. The presser foot on some sewing machines may need to be temporarily removed to slide the hoop under the needle. Be sure to leave enough room for the presser foot inside the embroidery hoop. For a stiffer ornament, remove embroidery from water as soon as fabric melts.

Enhance the rustic, woven look of burlap by removing groups of threads, creating stripes that allow the attached contrasting lining to show through. These place mats will add a comfortable, natural feel to the table. Experiment with removing both warp and weft threads for plaid or grid designs, or cut the fabric on the bias to create diagonal stripes. The finished burlap is very versatile— you can enlarge the finished area to make a table runner, pillow, or window treatment. Or, skip the lining for a lacy see-through effect.

ARTIST: NANCY WORRELL

burlap
place mats

Makes four place mats

1 Sew four stripes of zigzag and straight stitching along short ends of burlap to define the area for pulling threads. Divide the area between stitching into sections; pull individual threads to create a striped pattern by gently tugging on one end of the thread until the burlap becomes gathered along the line. Continue pulling on the thread, and push the gathers in the opposite direction so they slip off the held thread. Continue easing the thread out of the fabric until it is removed.

2 Fold back and press the short ends of the black fabric 1/2 " (1 cm) to the wrong side. Center the black fabric on the burlap piece, right sides together. Machine stitch long sides of burlap and fabric together. Turn to right side. Hand stitch the folded black edges to burlap.

3 Fringe the short edges of the burlap up to the hand stitching. Repeat for the remaining place mats.

VARIATIONS
Instead of lining the burlap with black fabric, leave off the backing for a sheer, lacelike place mat. After completing a pattern on the fabric by stitching and pulling, straight stitch approximately 1 " (3 cm) from all sides of the place mat; complete by fringing all edges to the stitching line.

MATERIALS
- four 12" x 14" (30 cm x 36 cm) burlap pieces
- four 11" x 14" (28 cm x 36 cm) black cotton fabric pieces
- red and black thread
- sewing machine
- general craft supplies

TIPS
Do a trial run on your sewing machine to determine if adjustments are needed for stitches or tension. Leave at least three threads together for each stripe as single threads tend to move or work their way out.

Display your favorite objects in this recessed frame made completely without nails. Balsa wood sandwiched between chipboard creates a deep niche large enough to hold coins, vintage metal type, or an antique brooch. Coarse, textural linen lines the mat, and toothpicks reinforce the hand-painted lattice-strip frame. Create a series of these architectural frames to display a collection of treasures. This project requires basic woodworking tools including a drill, fine-tooth saw, and miter box.

linen display frame

Makes one frame

1 Cut three 10 1/2" x 12" (27 cm x 30 cm) rectangles from the chipboard. Saw the balsa wood into two 12" (30 cm) and two 2 1/2" (6 cm) long pieces and trim the remaining piece to 1" x 2 1/2" (3 cm x 6 cm). Following layout diagram (see page 166), arrange the balsa pieces onto one chipboard rectangle, leaving a 2 1/2" x 3" (6 cm x 8 cm) area open. Trace the recess onto the chipboard, remove the balsa wood, and cut out the opening. Trace this opening onto a second chipboard rectangle, enlarge the opening by 1/2" (1 cm) on all four sides, and cut out to create mat board. Using wood glue, attach the balsa pieces to the remaining solid chipboard rectangle according to layout guide; next, glue the chipboard with the matching opening on top. Place entire assembly under heavy books and let dry overnight.

2 Enlarge niche template (see page 166) by 200%. Affix template to heavy white paper with spray adhesive and cut out template outline. Fold at dashed lines and tuck in triangle flaps. Glue to chipboard recess at back section of niche. In the remaining white paper, cut a 2 1/2" x 2 7/8" (6 cm x 7 cm) rectangle and glue to niche over opening to conceal mitered corners.

3 Cut two 12 1/2" (32 cm) and two 10 1/2" (27 cm) lattice strips for frame. Glue lattice strips to outer edge of chipboard assembly, allowing core recesses and lap joints to show at top and bottom. Clamp tightly with masking tape; let dry overnight. Drill three evenly spaced 1" (2 cm) deep holes in side strip at each corner, each just wide enough to fit a toothpick. Break toothpicks in half, dip the pointed end in glue, and lightly tap into each drilled hole. Let dry one hour and then sand each toothpick flush to frame. Paint and seal the frame as desired.

4 Press linen and lay flat on work surface. Tape down corners with masking tape. Brush contact cement on one face of remaining piece of chipboard; when tacky apply a second coat. Lightly spray linen with adhesive. Set the edge of the chipboard near edge of linen; slowly lower board glue side down onto linen surface. Turn right side out and smooth out wrinkles. Press linen to adhere. Diagonally trim corners 1/4" (.5 cm) from chipboard, fold in, and glue corners and edges. Cut an X in the fabric at mat opening, stopping 1/8" (.3 cm) before each corner. Fold triangles to back of mat and glue. Crisp the corners with a bone folder. Carefully ease completed mat into frame.

MATERIALS
- 24" x 30" (61 cm x 76 cm) 2-ply chipboard
- 30" x 4" x 3/4" (76 cm x 10 cm x 2 cm) balsa wood
- 8 1/2" x 11" (22 cm x 25 cm) heavy white paper
- 48" x 1 5/8" x 1/4" (122 cm x 1.5 cm x .5 cm) wood lattice
- 6 round toothpicks
- 13" x 14" (33 cm x 36 cm) coarse linen
- acrylic paint
- acrylic sealer
- wood glue
- contact cement
- spray adhesive
- bone folder
- layout guide and niche template (see page 166)
- drill, fine-tooth saw, miter box
- general craft supplies

TIPS
Test-fit all pieces in a dry run before gluing final assembly. Sand or shave pieces as needed to fit snugly.

These sumptuous pillows add a casual elegance to any décor. Bleaching velvet brings out depth and texture from the fabric. Lace or any loose weave fabric creates a mask for the bleach, leaving a rough, patterned finish when completed. A metallic stenciled design lends a sophisticated overlay. This project is an introduction to surface design techniques that can be applied to a wide variety of fabrics.

bleached-velvet
pillows

Makes one pillow

1 Wash and dry the fabric to remove sizing and preshrink. In a well-ventilated, protected area, adhere the lace to the right side of the velvet at top and bottom with masking tape. Lightly mist the bleach over the fabric. When the color has changed to the desired intensity, immediately soak the fabric in a weak mixture of white distilled vinegar and water to stop bleaching action. Wash and dry again.

2 Cut a square from the fabric for the front piece of the pillow, allowing 1/4" (.5 cm) extra on all sides for seam allowance. Cut two rectangles for the overlapping back pieces, each the entire width and three-quarters of the length of the front piece.

3 Enlarge the template on page 164 by 200%, and then trace it onto the polyester film stencil sheet and cut out interior areas with a craft knife. Tape the front piece of fabric, right side up, on a protected work surface. Center the stencil over the fabric and tape to secure. Using a vertical pouncing motion, apply metallic fabric paint with a stencil brush to the open areas of the stencil. Let dry. Set the paint according to manufacturer's directions.

4 With a sewing machine, finish one long edge of each backing piece of fabric. With right sides together, tack the two backing pieces to the front piece, inserting any desired pillow accents such as fringe or tassels, and overlapping the finished edges of the backing pieces in the middle to create a protected opening for the pillow form. Sew around pillow edge, leaving a 1/4" (.25 cm) seam. Clip corners, turn right side out, and insert pillow form.

VARIATION
Tint the bleached pattern with watered-down fabric paints to add more color.

MATERIALS

- one yard (.9 m) cotton velvet
- one yard (.9 m) lace
- chlorine bleach
- spray bottle
- white distilled vinegar
- stencil template (see page 164)
- polyester film stencil sheet
- metallic fabric paint
- stencil brush
- trim and tassels as desired
- 16" (41 cm) square pillow form
- general craft supplies

TIPS

Bleaching works best with natural fibers, so if you use synthetic fabric complete a test-swatch first. Apply the bleach outside in a well-ventilated area or wear a respirator. When cutting the stencil from the blank plastic sheet, use a piece of glass as a backing to facilitate cutting the curves. If ironing is recommended by the manufacturer to set the fabric paint, iron on the wrong side of the fabric to preserve the nap of the velvet.

ARTIST: PAULA GRASDAL

Let your love of one-of-a-kind table linens "develop" into these lovely pieces that are perfect for summer picnics. Like fireworks, these dramatic linens explode with starburst patterns created by scattering rice across pretreated fabric and exposing it to direct sunlight. Sun printing is an easy technique to complete alone or with your children, who will love watching these decorative designs bloom like flowers in the sun. The fabric has been specially treated turn a rich cyan blue where exposed to bright light.

sun-printed
picnic linens

Makes one tablecloth and four napkins

1 Working indoors with your lights off and windows shaded, remove the pretreated fabric from its protective pouch. Rough-cut the fabric into one 45" (114 cm) square for the table-cloth and four 18" (46 cm) squares for the napkins. Pin each square to a flat surface such as a corkboard or corrugated cardboard, then slip each piece into a large black trash bag until you're ready to expose the fabric.

2 Take one of the napkin boards to a sunny outdoor location. Pour 1/4 cup (60 ml) of the rice onto the middle of the fabric and, working quickly, spread out the grains into a sunburst pattern. Set the timer to your pretested exposure (5 to 10 minutes on a sunny summer day; 15 to 20 minutes on a clear winter day). When the timer sounds, cover fabric with a blanket to stop the exposure. Tilt the board to shed the rice.

3 Bring the fabric back indoors to dim light and immediately rinse in the sink until the water runs clear. Dry flat on paper towels or newsprint to protect your work surface and re-rinse the fabric if the paper shows traces of blue.

4 Repeat steps 2 and 3 to print the other napkins. Follow the same steps for the tablecloth, but use 2 cups (480 ml) rice; rinse the fabric in a washing machine and tumble dry. To pre-vent white spots on the final pattern, make sure the washer is free of any powdered deter-gent residue.

5 Iron each piece and trim with a rotary cutter to even the edges and square corners. Fringe the edges by machine-stitching 1/2" (1 cm) from all sides of the fabric and then pulling out cross threads to the stitching line.

VARIATIONS

Try other pantry items such as dried beans or grains, or use botanicals such as leaves, branches, flow-ers, or ferns to create earthy and elegant patterns. To coordinate with your decorating scheme, experi-ment with other distinctive shapes such as starfish or lace doilies. Using the finished material, create custom-designed throw pillows, curtains, and even tote bags.

MATERIALS
- 2.25 yards (2 m) 45" (114 cm) wide sensitized white twill fabric
- 1 pound (.45 kg) white rice
- sewing machine
- general craft supplies

TIPS
Try one or two trial runs with fabric swatches, as the exposure time can vary due to the season or brightness of the day. The pre-treated fabric is light sensitive, so don't remove it from its light-proof plastic pouch until you are ready to begin. Work quickly between steps to completely control the exposure.

ARTIST: NANCY WORRELL

Four shades of satin ribbon woven together create the fabric for this unusual and elegant handbag. The fusible interfacing holds the ribbons together and adds strength to the purse. This project is an easy introduction to weaving and allows creative freedom in choosing the color palette. Design coordinating handbags in spring pastels or jewel tones for bridesmaids, or pick natural hues for a more subdued ensemble. Or, sew this delightful purse for your favorite little girl's first handbag.

woven ribbon
handbag

Makes one purse

1 Place the rectangle of interfacing on an ironing board, adhesive side up. Cut six 15" (38 cm) lengths of white ribbon and five 15" (38 cm) lengths of pink ribbon. Pin vertically in alternating colors to create the warp of the weaving, leaving 1/2" (1 cm) interfacing uncovered on each side for seam allowance.

2 Trim blue and green ribbon into ten 8" (20 cm) lengths each for weft of weaving. Beginning 1/2" (1 cm) from the top edge of the interfacing, weave the weft ribbons horizontally across the pink and white warp ribbons in an alternating over and under basket-weave pattern, pinning each row immediately to the next.

3 Following interfacing manufacturer's instructions, fuse the ribbon weaving to the interfacing. Machine-stitch along the outside edge of the weaving to secure all ribbons. Trim overhanging ribbons to the interfacing if necessary.

4 Fold the weaving in half, rights sides together, and stitch side seams with a 1/2" (1 cm) seam allowance. Fold lining fabric in half, right sides together, and also stitch side seams with a 1/2" (1 cm) seam allowance. Cut two 12" (30 cm) lengths of white ribbon for handles and baste to right side of top edges of the bag, aligning each end with a white strip of warp ribbon. With right sides together, stitch the lining and bag together at the top edge, leaving a small opening for turning. Turn right side out and fold lining into bag. Slip-stitch opening and press.

5 Make a small bow from the remaining white ribbon and hand-stitch to the front of the bag. Stitch a dot of hook-and-loop fastener to the inside top of the bag to secure.

MATERIALS

- 2 1/4 yards (2.1 m) of 5/8" (1.5 cm) pink, blue, and green satin ribbons
- 3 2/3 yards (3.4 m) of 5/8" (1.5 cm) white satin ribbon
- 7 7/8" x 14 3/4" (20 cm x 38 cm) fusible interfacing
- 7 7/8" x 14 3/4" (20 cm x 38 cm) white satin fabric
- white dot of hook-and-loop fastener
- sewing machine
- general craft supplies

ARTIST: ELAINE SCHMIDT

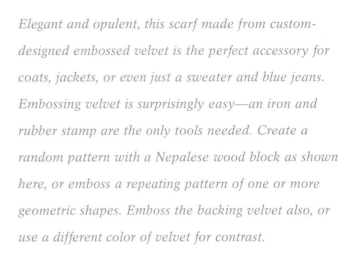

Elegant and opulent, this scarf made from custom-designed embossed velvet is the perfect accessory for coats, jackets, or even just a sweater and blue jeans. Embossing velvet is surprisingly easy—an iron and rubber stamp are the only tools needed. Create a random pattern with a Nepalese wood block as shown here, or emboss a repeating pattern of one or more geometric shapes. Emboss the backing velvet also, or use a different color of velvet for contrast.

embossed
velvet scarf

Makes one scarf

1 Set the iron to wool/cotton setting with steam off. On an ironing board, place the front piece of velvet nap-side-down over the patterned portion of the stamp. Spray the back of the fabric with water until damp. Place iron over the stamp and hold stationary with even pressure for 15 to 20 seconds. For an even design, use the area of the iron that doesn't have steam holes if possible. If your iron has nonstick coating, you may move the iron slowly over the surface of the velvet while embossing if stamp image is larger than the surface area of your iron. Repeat as desired.

2 Finish all edges of front and back pieces of velvet with a hemming or zigzag stitch. With right sides facing, sew front and back pieces of velvet together with a 1/2" (1 cm) seam allowance, leaving a 5" (13 cm) section open on one side. Turn right side out through the opening and slip-stitch closed.

VARIATIONS

Combine with velvet-bleaching technique (see page 84) to add more distinctive texture to the final scarf. Emboss the fabric with coiled wire, coat hangers, or metal cookie cutters. Create a wider scarf for an elegant evening wrap.

MATERIALS

- 48" x 9" (122 cm x 23 cm) length velvet for embossing
- 48" x 9" (122 cm x 23 cm) length velvet for backing
- rubber stamp or wood block
- iron and ironing board
- spray water bottle
- sewing machine
- general craft supplies

TIPS

Test-emboss velvet scraps to check for timing and embossing effect since velvets made from different fibers yield varying results. When sewing velvet, the pile occasionally will get caught in the seam, causing a flat spot in the nap. Use a straight pin to pull the pile out from the seam.

ARTIST: MARTHA THURLOW

Simple machine stitches combine to create contemporary geometric shapes on this innovative pillow design. Single repeats of decorative stitches grouped and aligned to an invisible grid transform the character of the fabric, and the playful looped edging echoes the lighthearted machine embroidery. Experiment with all of the custom stitches available on your machine to make unique shapes and patterns. The finished pillow features an envelope backing for easy removal of the pillow form.

stitch-art pillow

Makes one pillow

1 Cut a 9" x 16 1/2" (23 cm x 42 cm) rectangle from both the camel and white fabrics for the pillow fronts. Cut one 9" x 16 1/2" (23 cm x 42 cm) camel rectangle and one 13" x 16 1/2" (33 cm x 42 cm) white rectangle for the pillow back pieces.

2 Machine-stitch front pieces together along a long edge, making a 3/4" (2 cm) seam. Press seam open. On right side of fabric, topstitch down each side of seam with matching thread. On each back piece, press one long edge 3/4" (2 cm) to wrong side and stitch down. Lay the back pieces right side up and overlap the hemmed edges, camel piece on top, so overall back dimensions match the size of the pillow front. Tack the two back pieces together at the overlap.

3 Iron the stabilizer to the wrong side of pillow front following manufacturer's directions. Transfer embroidery motifs to the right side, using layout diagram and transfer paper or draw a design directly on the fabric with a chalk pencil.

4 Using your sewing machine's decorative stitches, machine-embroider motifs: Use a wide satin stitch to create the Greek key pattern. Satin-stitch the ladder pole, starting at middle with a wide stitch and tapering to a point at each end, and use graduated widths for rungs to correspond to pole tapering. Stitch two scallops back to back to make the coffee bean shape. Satin-stitch the dots by hand. Remove stabilizer when through.

5 To finish assembling the pillow, machine-baste a length of fringe to pillow front along each solid-color edge. Pin back and front right sides together with camel and white sections back to back. Tack at center seams to prevent shifting. Stitch 1/2" (1 cm) from edge all around. Clip the corners, turn right side out, and insert the pillow form.

MATERIALS

- 1/2 yard (1/2 m) camel 45" (114 cm) wide wool melton cloth
- 1/2 yard winter white 45" wide wool melton cloth
- sewing threads to match fabrics
- iron-on tearaway stabilizer
- four motifs template (see page 165)
- machine embroidery thread in purple, pink, avocado, and mauve
- 1 yard (1 m) satin loop fringe
- 16" (41 cm) square pillow form
- sewing machine
- general craft supplies

TIP

Iron stabilizer to a wool scrap to use for practice stitching.

ARTIST: MICHIO RYAN

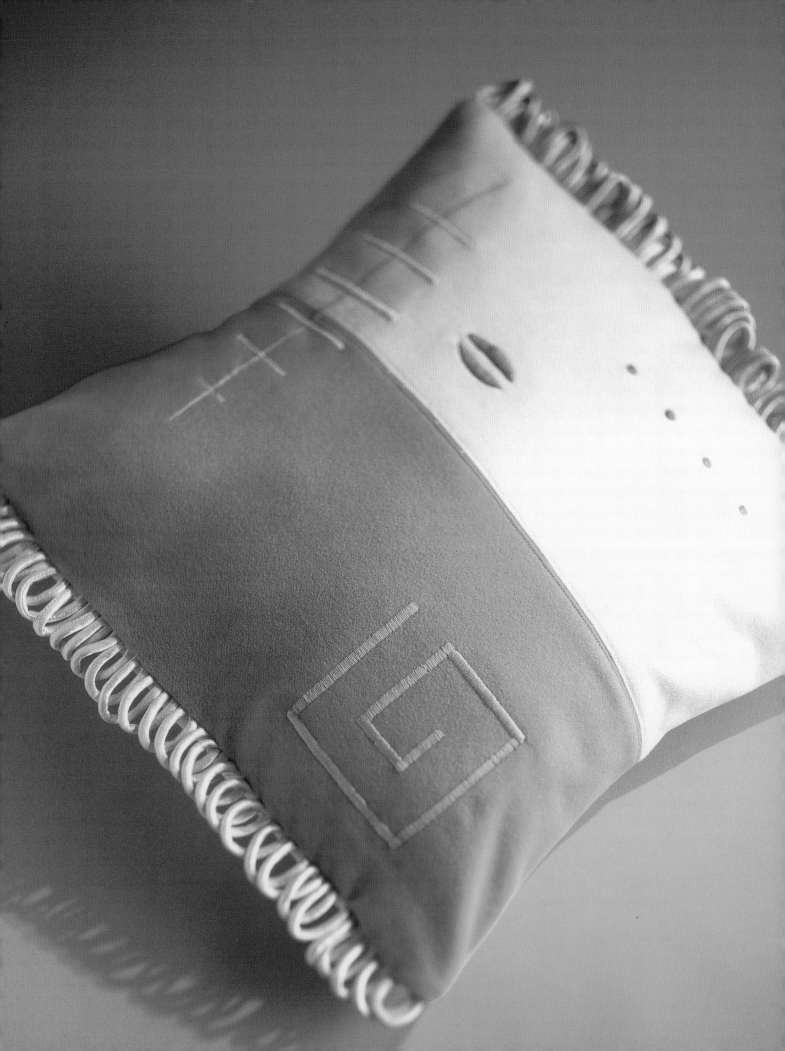

ceramic & glass projects

Mosaic has been a popular decorative art throughout the ages. Here's an easy way to create a charming address plaque using glass tiles and premixed latex grout. Mosaic tiles can be purchased in small, square pieces or cut into irregular shapes to add an artistic air to the final piece. If you don't have the woodworking tools to create a frame from plywood and molding, use a ready-made picture frame and have a woodworking shop cut a piece of plywood to fit the interior.

mosaic
address plaque

Makes one plaque

1 Cut wood molding to size, miter corners, and attach to plywood base with finishing nails and wood glue. Paint or stain molding as desired.

2 Sketch your desired tile design on a sheet of tracing paper. With carbon paper, transfer the design to the plywood base. Using tile nippers, clip tiles to fit desired pattern, setting them on the tracing paper sketch to organize. Allow up to 1/8" (.32 cm) space between tiles.

3 Working in one small area at a time, apply tile adhesive to the wood surface with a v-notch trowel or glue spreader according to manufacturer's directions. Transfer the cut tile pieces, smooth side up, from the paper template to the adhesive. Set for 5–6 hours.

4 Protect the finished frame molding with quick release tape. Spread premixed grout over the tiles with a grout float or flat-blade spreader tool and work into open spaces until grout is level with tiles. Let set 20–30 minutes. Wipe away excess grout with a damp sponge. Let dry completely. Remove tape and polish tiles using a soft cloth or damp paper towel.

MATERIALS

- 5/8" (1.5 cm) thick plywood, cut to desired size
- wood molding for edging
- finishing nails
- wood glue
- paint or stain
- mosaic glass tiles
- tile nippers
- mosaic tile adhesive
- v-notch trowel or glue spreader
- premixed latex nonsanded grout
- grout float or flat-blade spreader tool
- grout sponge
- general craft supplies

VARIATIONS

Add a bit of acrylic paint to the grout to tint. Instead of tiling your address number, make a mosaic of your family name or initials, and hang on your front door.

TIPS

Wear safety glasses and gloves when cutting tile with nippers. Apply the tile adhesive to the wood base in areas delineated by the sketched design to facilitate transferring the tiled pattern from the paper sketch to the final project. Premixed, nonsanded latex grout is appropriate for grout lines that are 1/8" (.32 cm) or less. For wider grout lines, use sanded grout following manufacturer's instructions for preparation. To prevent warping of thinner wood substrates, prime wood first with mosaic tile primer.

ARTIST: BRIDGET HEIDI NEWFELL

"Beach pebbles" made from polymer clay form these chunky and col-orful napkin rings. Create irregular pebbles in solid and marbleized colors, and thread alternating faux pearls on the wire to continue the sea-worthy theme. This is a simple and easy introduction to the versatality of polymer clay. Combine these whimsical rings with napkins stamped in a nautical pattern (see page 78) for a coordinated gift set.

beach-pebble
napkin rings

Makes four napkin rings

1 Cut translucent clay into four equal sections. Condition each piece by warming in your hands and kneading until it is smooth and pliable. Set aside on protected surface. Cut a small section from one color of polymer clay about the size of a large pea. Blend the colored clay into the translucent by repeatedly flattening the clays into a rectangle and folding it back on itself in thirds, rotating 90° each time so folds are in opposite directions. Mix until color is uniform. Repeat for other three colors, saving the white clay for later.

2 Mix a small amount of glitter into each of the four tinted clay pieces by making a depression in the clay, pouring the glitter in, then folding clay on itself repeatedly until the glitter is evenly distrib-uted.

3 Create the solid beads by rolling each piece of tinted clay into a short, thick log. Cut pieces in half. Set aside one half of each tint. Roll each remaining piece into a thinner log about 4" (10 cm) long and cut into four equal pieces. Form each small piece into a pebble shape by rolling and gently pressing between your palms. You should now have sixteen beads. Create the bead hole by spin-ning a toothpick between thumb and first finger as you push it through the bead to make a drilling action. Remove the toothpick with a reverse drilling action while pulling it out. Set beads aside.

4 To make marbleized beads, roll each of the reserved pieces of tinted clay into a short log about 3" (8 cm) long. Cut four small blocks of white clay, condition slightly, and roll each block into a thin snake about 3" (8 cm) long. Lay a white piece on one of the tinted logs and roll together until they form a new log about 8" (20 cm) long. Fold in half and twist one end 6 to 8 times. Roll the log again until it is 8" (20 cm) long. Again fold in half and twist 6 to 8 times. Cut the log into four equal pieces. Roll, twist, and form each piece into pebble shapes, adding bead holes as directed above. Repeat for remaining colors.

5 Line a shiny metal baking pan with white paper, place the beads on the pan, and bake the beads according to manufacturer's directions. Ventilate the area well while baking.

6 Cut a piece of wire 11" (28 cm) long. Bend wire to 90° two inches (5 cm) from one end. Beginning with a marbleized bead, string 8 clay beads with alternating pearl beads. Thread straight wire end through first bead and pull to form threaded beads into a tight circle. Clip straight end to 1 1/2" (4 cm) and wrap tightly four times around inner wire between first bead and faux pearl. Cut wire and pinch with pliers. Repeat wrapping with wire on other end. Repeat process to create three more napkin rings.

MATERIALS

- 2 oz. blocks polymer clay in white, blue, turquoise, medium green, and lime green
- 4 oz. translucent clay
- fine or ultrafine iridescent glitter
- 32 round faux-pearl beads
- 44" (112 cm) 24-gauge galvanized steel
- general craft supplies

TIPS

Never reuse pans, cutting boards, or utensils for food preparation after using them with polymer clay. Make sure there is good ventilation while baking the clay. Wear latex gloves to prevent fingerprints on the clay, and to give a smooth, matte surface to the beads. Clean raw clay film from tools and hands with rubbing alcohol. Clean the finished napkin rings with a damp cloth; do not soak in any solution. Protect your work surface from oils in the clay with layers of plastic wrap and white paper. Do not overmix the marbleized beads or you will lose the color variations.

ARTIST: ANNE RUSSELL

Store your favorite treasures in this beautifully painted glass box. Decorate a collection of glass boxes to hold cotton balls and potpourri in your bathroom, or embellish a larger container as a jewelry box. The swirled lines and patterns are easy to create using a Color Shaper®, a decorative painting tool that you customize by cutting the edge in random notches. The Color Shaper® removes the wet glaze in patterns as it is swept through the translucent glass paint, creating new colors where the paints overlap.

painted
glass box

Makes one box

1 Cut a random pattern of notches into the Color Shaper® with a craft knife.

2 Thin turquoise glass paint with a drop of water to extend working time. Apply paint to the glass box cover with the soft bristle brush. Form wavy stripes through the wet paint with the Color Shaper®, using firm pressure. Continue for all outside areas of the box, working one section at a time. Following paint manufacturer's directions, heat-set the piece in your oven.

3 Repeat step 2 for yellow glass paint, creating stripes in the opposite direction with the same Color Shaper®; heat-set again according to manufacturer's recommendations.

4 Attach green glass accents with a clear-drying glass or porcelain cement. Let dry.

VARIATIONS
Custom-paint glass canisters for see-through storage of beans, rice, and other grains in the kitchen.

MATERIALS
- clear glass storage container
- turquoise and yellow glass paint
- 3" (8 cm) curved Color Shaper®
- soft bristle brush
- 12 flat-backed glass accents in green
- clear-drying glass glue or porcelain cement
- general craft supplies

TIPS
Only paint the outside surface of the glass box to keep the inside food-safe.

ARTIST: PAULA DESIMONE,
PAINTING GLASS WITH THE COLOR SHAPER

Embellish a terra cotta pot using simple cake-decorating tools and extra heavy gel medium to create this aged, iced planter. As you become more skillful with the decorating tools, you'll want to create more complex patterns. The paint colors are based on those typically used in Victorian Majolica, a type of naturalistic molded pottery prized by collectors. Package a finished pot with bulbs or a garden trowel as a lovely gift for a green-thumbed friend.

iced
flower pot

Makes one pot

1 Lightly sketch a design on the pot to mark placement of gel accents.

2 Fill the cake-decorating tube with extra heavy gel medium. With the desired tip attached, add icing accents to the pot following the sketched pattern using a squirt, twist, and lift motion. When completed, set aside to thoroughly dry. Depending on your climate, this can take up to a week.

3 Paint the outside and top edge of the pot with the dark blue acrylic paint. Let dry. Paint over the dark blue with a light application of turquoise paint, wiping off in relief sections to expose the dark color underneath; let dry. Paint the inside of the pot with pink paint.

4 Finish with an overall application of spray acrylic varnish following manufacturer's directions. Let dry completely.

VARIATION
After mastering basic cake-decorating techniques, create roses, leaves, and basket-weaving patterns on subsequent pots.

MATERIALS
• terra cotta flower pot
• extra-heavy gel medium
• cake-decorating tube and tips
• craft acrylic paints in dark blue, turquoise, and pink
• spray acrylic gloss varnish
• general craft supplies

TIPS
Practice making shapes with each decorating tip before applying gel medium to the pot. Clean the decorating tips with soap and water immediately after use and reserve for craft use only. The decorating tube should be discarded after use.

ARTIST: JANE ASPER

Completing ceramic pieces is no longer a daunting task with this non-firing method. And this unique vase becomes functional as well as beautiful with the addition of a water-repellent coating inside. Any piece of bisqueware can be finished with these ceramic tints and sealer—use them to create unique groups of coordinating vases, bowls, or planters. The ceramic paints can be applied lightly for a translucent wash of color, heavily for more opaque color, or in layers for even more coloring options.

painted
bisqueware vase

Makes one vase

1 Wipe vase with damp sponge to remove dust. Paint inside of vase with water-repellent coating following manufacturer's directions.

2 Apply a solid coat of primary blue paint to entire vase with foam brush. Sponge on the remaining colors in uneven, random patches. Apply the sparkle tints as highlights. Gently apply gold antiquing gel with a foam brush. Wipe away random areas to distress finish. Let dry thoroughly.

3 Lightly sand areas if desired to further age finish. Spray the outside with ceramic sealer. Allow to dry.

MATERIALS

- one bisqueware vase
- water repellent coating for ceramics
- non-firing translucent natural ceramic tints in primary blue, patina blue, patina green, jade sparkle, tan sparkle
- metallic gold water-based antiquing gel
- ceramic sealer
- general craft supplies

TIPS

If the foam brush does not fit easily inside the vase, pour the water-repellent coating inside and swirl until absorbed to seal. For exterior surface lightly wipe away tinted or gelled areas to create highlights. Cut a kitchen sponge into pieces, and use a different piece to apply each translucent color.

ARTIST: LIVIA MCREE

These custom drawer pulls add just the right accent to a room's furnishings and can make an old piece of furniture seem new again. Choose a stamp that will complement your decorating theme. Brushing or sponging the glaze to the rubber stamp each results in different textures in the stamped image. If you don't have access to a kiln, bring the glazed pieces to a commercial pottery studio or rent kiln time from a professional ceramic artist.

ARTIST: MARTHA THURLOW

glazed-ceramic
drawer pulls

Makes six drawer pulls

1 Working from light to dark colors, select the base color of glaze and brush or sponge one coat on drawer pulls. Let dry. Sponge a second color of glaze, and let dry.

2 Paint or sponge glaze onto the printing area of your selected rubber stamp. Avoid using too much glaze to keep stamped image sharp and to prevent stamp from slipping when applied to the pottery. Stamp drawer pulls with images as desired. Add dots, lines, and other details with fine brushes dipped in glaze. Let dry completely.

3 Apply a coat of clear glaze. Wipe the bottom of the pulls with a damp sponge to remove any drips; let dry. Fire the drawer pulls and cone 05 in an electric kiln one hour at low temperature, one hour at medium temperature, and then at high temperature until cone 05 melts enough to bend in half. Remove the drawer pulls when cool to the touch.

4 Epoxy threaded rod in place on each drawer pull. When dry, attach to furniture with screws.

Materials
- six bisqueware drawer pulls
- rubber stamps
- colored and clear glazes
- cone 05
- electric kiln
- threaded rods and screws to fit
- epoxy glue
- general craft supplies

TIP
Practice stamping on scrap pottery until you determine the correct amount of glaze and pressure to apply to rubber stamp.

Individualize plain wineglasses with this effortless and versatile lamination technique to create a singular dining experience. Mix and match fabrics to fashion a mood or to coordinate with decor or place settings. Present the glasses with a bottle of champagne or fine wine for an impressive and personal housewarming, shower, or wedding gift, or have a group of friends each make one glass to produce a personalized collection for a new bride. You can also substitute paper for fabric with this method.

fabric-laminated
wineglasses

Makes two glasses

1 Turn wineglass upside down and clean base with glass cleaner. Paint a thin, even coat of decoupage medium to the bottom of glass base with a foam brush. Rough-cut a square of fabric that is larger than the glass base and apply the right side to the decoupage medium on the glass. Starting from the center and moving to the outside of the base, gently smooth out bubbles in the fabric with damp fingertips.

2 Apply a second coat of decoupage medium to the fabric and let dry one hour. Trim the excess fabric from the base of the glass with a single-edge razor blade.

3 Apply a third coat of decoupage medium evenly over fabric base and let dry one hour. Sand gently with a sanding sponge. Remove dust with a dry cloth. Repeat 6–8 times, until fabric is firmly laminated to glass base. Clean any excess decoupage medium from glass with a single-edge razor blade.

VARIATION

Before applying fabric to glass, paint names on the fabric in calligraphy (or print on handmade paper with permanent ink) and use the glasses as placecards for a dinner party. Guests can take them home as favors.

MATERIALS
- 2 wine glasses
- decoupage medium
- fabric
- general craft supplies

TIPS
Finished glasses should only be hand-washed in warm water with a mild soap.

ARTIST: MARIA TESTA

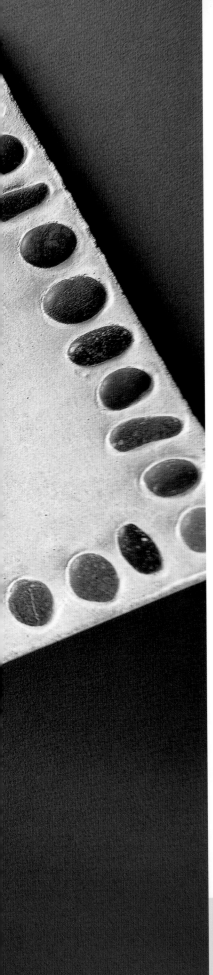

Indoors or out, create the impression of a European garden with these unique ornamental stepping stones. Design a patio path or garden walk using the easy-to-make mosaics of smooth and colorful Mexican pebbles, or cast the number of your street address for an attractive architectural addition to your home's façade. Indoors, display these pieces singly or in a group, or, mount one on a wrought-iron base for a distinctive side table.

pebbled
garden stones

Makes one stepping stone

1 Prepare concrete according to manufacturer's directions. Transfer the mix to the mold; smooth surface with putty knife. Shake mold gently back and forth to level surface.

2 Working quickly, lay the stones on the surface of the wet concrete. After entire design is placed, lightly press the stones partway into mix. Go around a second time to press in stones a bit further. Shake mold back and forth gently to smooth surface of concrete and settle stones. Press in each stone once more, until concrete covers its widest point.

3 Following manufacturer's instructions, let concrete stone dry undisturbed to cure for 24 hours. Cover stone with wet cloth and continue curing for another 2 days or until the surface is hard. Remove stone from mold. Wearing a particle mask and goggles, smooth the edges of the stone with a sponge sanding block. Remove the dusty residue from surface with a kitchen scrubber.

MATERIALS
- 7 pounds (1 bag) craft concrete
- 5 pounds mixed Mexican pebbles
- 12" mold (square or round)
- general craft supplies

VARIATIONS
Try broken pottery or plates instead of pebbles. Use stone color pigments to vary the color of the cement.

ARTIST: DAWN ANDERSON

TIP
For ease of design and quick transfer of the pebbles to the wet cement, first make a template by tracing the outline of the mold onto paper. Divide the template into quarters and transfer the quadrant guidelines to the rim of the mold using a permanent pen. Use the template for preliminary arranging of the pebbles.

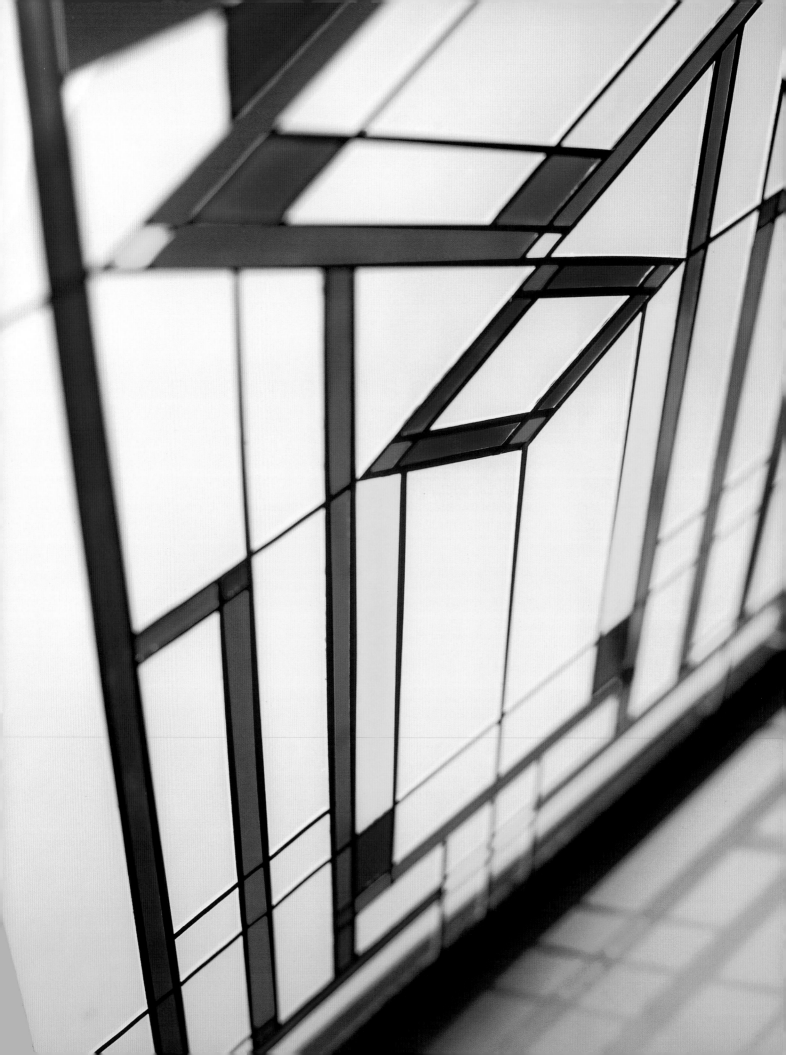

Turn a simple black frame into a faux stained-glass sun-catcher with translucent glass paint and thin black graphic arts tape. As a variation, paint a stained glass matte around a glass floating frame or decorate a front-door window for a striking first impression. A template for this clean and elegant pattern, inspired by the designs of Frank Lloyd Wright, is provided on page 167.

painted stained-glass
w i n d o w

Makes one window

1 Photocopy the pattern on page 167 at 400%.

2 Clean both sides of the glass. Lay the glass on top of the pattern square with the design, and secure with masking tape at corners.

3 Following the copied pattern, paint all areas keyed red with the red glass paint. Let dry according to manufacturer's directions. Repeat with remaining keyed areas and paint, allowing glass to dry between colors.

4 When completely dry, separate the pattern from the glass. Turn the glass over and realign to the template, painted side down. Reattach the corners with masking tape. Following pattern lines, apply the black tape to the right side of the glass, concealing the paint edges. Tape all vertical lines first, then horizontal, and then diagonal. Trim the tape neatly with a craft knife and miter-cut the diamond points. Burnish the tape lightly with a craft stick.

5 Apply silicone sealer to the inside rabbet edge of frame. Place the glass in the frame, taped side down, and wipe off any excess silicone. If available, fold the frame's easel anchors down against the glass or install new glazier's points to secure. Let dry overnight.

MATERIALS

- 16" x 20" (41 cm x 51 cm) narrow black frame with glass
- no-bake transparent glass paint in blue, red, green, and yellow
- pattern (see page 167)
- flat paintbrushes
- 3/8" (1 cm) black matte graphic arts tape
- clear silicone sealer
- glazier's points (optional)
- general craft supplies

TIPS

For straight painted edges, use the side of a piece of cardboard as a guide: simply lay a strip of cardboard along the pattern line and run your brush along the edge. Use a single-edge razor blade to correct painting errors. The tape added later will conceal small errors and provide clean, sharp lines to the final project

ARTIST: ELIZABETH CAMERON

Recycle your broken pots into lively and beautiful frames and bring a patio garden feel indoors. Make a plaster frame as a base for the mosaic to enhance the irregular, casual look of terracotta, or revitalize an old frame with this simple technique. This is a wonderful frame to highlight images of flowers, landscapes, or other natural images, and it will enhance many decorating schemes, from European country to American Southwestern.

terracotta
mosaic frame

Makes one frame

1 Follow manufacturer's instructions to mix craft plaster and pour into mold. Allow to harden; remove from mold. Cure plaster according to manufacturer's recommendations.

2 Use tile nippers to even edges of terracotta pieces if desired. Adhere terracotta to the front of the frame with tile adhesive or silicone sealant. Let dry completely.

3 According to manufacturer's directions, mix sanded grout with water in a disposable container until it has a fudge-like consistency. Wearing rubber gloves, spread grout into spaces between pieces with a grout float or wet sponge, making sure to press grout firmly into cracks. Follow with another clean, wet sponge to wipe off excess grout. Allow to dry.

4 Sand rough edges with sandpaper. Clean frame with a damp cloth.

5 Adhere photo corners to the back of the frame to hold a picture or photograph.

MATERIALS
- craft plaster
- picture frame mold
- broken terracotta pot
- tile nippers
- silicone sealant or tile adhesive
- sanded tile grout
- grout float
- photo corners
- general craft supplies

VARIATION
Substitute glass pebbles, broken china or tiles, shells, coins, stained glass, or pebbles for the terracotta pieces.

TIPS
To break terracotta, wrap a pot in several layers of newspaper, enclose in a plastic bag, and tap pot gently with a hammer until it is broken into pieces of the desired size. Moisten the surface of the terracotta before applying grout so less grout adheres to mosaic pieces. Spread grout at an angle to the terracotta edges to fill in spaces without forming air pockets. When grout is partially dry, wipe with a damp sponge to even grout lines and smooth rough edges.

ARTIST: KELLEY TAYLOR

Etching adds a frosted finish to smooth glass. It is combined here with other techniques to make exquisite coasters. For an original design, use stencils on two pieces of glass, then encase any flat memento such as pressed flowers, postage stamps, picture collages, or vintage drink recipes between them. Seal the edges with metal foil tape that comes in a variety of widths. The tape can be adhered flush with the glass edges or folded over the front and back surfaces to create a frame.

etched-glass
coasters

ARTIST: LIVIA MCREE

Makes one coaster

1 Cut the glass to size, or have a retail glass supplier custom-cut them. Sand all edges so they are not sharp.

2 Using an iron set on medium-low, iron the freezer paper shiny side down to one piece of glass to adhere, or peel away the backing of self-stick shelving paper and press to the glass to seal. Sketch the desired design on the paper. Trace the lines with a craft knife and remove the portions that will be etched. Paint a thick and even coat of etching cream to exposed areas with a foam brush, and let sit according to manufacturer's instructions (usually about 5–10 minutes). Thoroughly rinse off cream and peel away remaining paper.

3 Clean both sides of each glass with glass cleaner. When completely dry, arrange items to be encased on the bottom piece. Place second glass piece carefully on top. Hold glass pieces firmly together and tack together on adjoining sides with transparent tape. Run length of the metal tape over the other two sides, centered over the glass edges. Peel off transparent tape, and adhere the metal tape to remaining edges. Trim metal tape and fold corners neatly. Burnish lightly with cloth to seal.

VARIATIONS
Experiment with different glass widths and types for special effects. Etch both sides of the top glass for layered designs. These coasters are slightly oversized to accommodate large glasses and mugs. Create different sizes and shapes to coordinate with your glassware.

TIP
Etching cream is very caustic, so follow the manufacturer's directions carefully.

MATERIALS
- two 4 1/2" x 4 1/2" (11 cm x 11 cm) glass pieces (clear or stained)
- freezer paper or vinyl self-stick shelving paper
- etching cream
- metal foil tape
- pressed flowers
- decorative paper
- general craft supplies

Just as a patchwork quilt is pieced together from scraps, these beautiful stained-glass napkin rings are created from a mosaic of scrap glass. This project assumes some basic knowledge of glass cutting and soldering skills. Leave the solder its natural silver color to match a cool color palette or rub with solder patina to create a copper or other warm tone. These napkin rings make a perfect wedding gift or add festive accent to your own table. Be sure to light candles while dining to catch the sparkling reflection in the stained glass rings.

ARTIST: JACQUELINE WINCH

stained-glass
napkin rings

Makes four napkin rings

1 Cut glass into pieces approximately 1/2" (1 cm) square. Wrap the edges of each piece with copper foil.

2 Spray the cardboard core from toilet paper roll or plastic wrap with spray adhesive. When glue is tacky, position a double or triple row of glass pieces in a ring shape around the core. Apply flux to edges of glass with flux brush. Tack-solder each piece to its neighbor by applying a dot of solder at joints. Remove cardboard core.

3 Finish soldering the inside of the ring, keeping solder lines neat and flat. For the outside of the napkin ring, raise a bead with the solder for a decorative effect. Clean ring well. Rub with patina solution and terry towel if desired, cleaning again to remove patina solution. Polish with stained glass polishing compound and a terry towel until glass and solder gleam. Repeat for remaining napkin rings.

Materials
- stained glass scraps
- glass cutter
- copper foil
- flux and flux brush
- soldering iron
- solder (50/50 tin to lead)
- solder patina (optional)
- terry towel (optional)
- cardboard roll core from toilet paper or plastic wrap
- spray adhesive
- finishing wax
- general craft supplies

TIP
It is not necessary to cut glass into perfect squares, as solder will fill gaps. After mastering basic soldering techniques, use quickset solder on the outside of the rings for more decorative soldering effects. Solder will oxidize quickly into a naturally darker color. Cover solder joints with a clear, high-gloss fingernail polish to retard oxidation if desired.

Carving and glazing a slate frame creates an impressive piece for showcasing a precious photograph. The flower design, provided as a template, accents the natural, outdoorsy feel of the stone frame. Engraving the slate surface requires a high-speed rotary tool and specialized tips, but the result is a unique textured design not easily duplicated by other means. For best results, use acrylic paints that are specially created for painting outdoor concrete and terra cotta.

engraved slate frame

Makes one frame

1 Transfer design from page 166 to the face of the square frame with a water-soluble marking pen. If necessary, enlarge or reduce the template to fit your chosen frame size.

2 Using the rotary tool according to manufacturer's directions, carve the design in the slate frame. Only a light touch is needed; allow the speed of the tool to do the work. Use the silicon carbide tip for large areas of the design, and use diamond point tip to carve tiny detailed areas.

3 Mix one part clear glaze to one part acrylic paint to create color glaze for painting. Fill in the carved design with the colored glazes and paintbrush. Allow to dry.

4 If desired, create a transparent color wash by mixing two parts clear glaze with one part of selected acrylic paint. Apply to entire frame with a small sea sponge; let dry.

5 Apply a finishing coat of clear glaze to front and back surfaces of frame. Let dry thoroughly.

VARIATION
Personalize the frame by engraving names, phrases, or dates. The rotary tool can be used to carve other stone surfaces such as terracotta, quarry tile, and sandstone.

TIPS
Wear safety goggles and a dust mask when using the rotary tool. Use a flexible shaft attachment on your rotary tool for more precise control.

MATERIALS
- square slate frame
- high-speed rotary tool with pointed silicon carbide grinding stone tip and diamond point tip
- water-soluble marking pen
- acrylic paint for outdoor concrete and terra cotta in white, cream, yellow, brown, pink, dark green, light green, and sky blue
- clear glaze for outdoor concrete and terra cotta
- template (see page 166)
- general craft supplies

ARTIST: BRENDA SPITZER

A wonderful shower or housewarming gift, these hand-painted daisy glasses are perfect for summertime margaritas on the porch. Or, use them to serve a refreshing sorbet or fruit salad at a patio luncheon. This flower design is easy to create with just three colors, or change the palette to make black-eyed Susans or gerbera daisies. Expand on the design by adding polka dots or other colored accents. Many brands of paints are created for glass painting—read the manufacturer's recommendations before beginning.

daisy-painted
margarita glasses

Makes four glasses

1 Wash the glasses well with soap and water; rinse and dry thoroughly. With a soft, lint-free cloth, wipe glasses with a small amount of rubbing alcohol.

2 Begin creating daisy petals by painting an "X" using a round brush and white paint. Fill in additional petals between original strokes. Repeat for remaining daisies. Let dry for one hour.

3 Using the rounded brush handle, paint a yellow dot in the center of each daisy. Paint the flower stems with a thin liner brush and green paint. With a round brush, paint the base edge of each glass with a green border. Paint alternating stripes of green and white on each glass stem. Create single white petals on each base by using the brush handle dipped in a small amount of white paint. Press the end to the glass, then pull lightly away to make the petal shape. Let glasses dry for one hour.

4 Finish each design with clear gloss glaze. Let glasses cure for ten days before use.

VARIATION
Paint a coordinated design on a glass pitcher for a complete beverage service.

MATERIALS
- four margarita glasses
- nonfiring glass paints in white, yellow, green, and clear gloss glaze
- round watercolor brush
- thin liner brush
- general craft supplies

ARTIST: NIKKI ST. MARY-KINGSLEY

TIP
Avoid drip marks by using only a small amount of paint on the brush. Hand-washing the completed glassware is recommended.

This beaded mosaic frame is deceptively simple to create by glu-ing prethreaded beads in rows and removing the thread after the adhesive has set. Using prethreaded beads saves time, but you can thread your own selection of beads if desired. The shape of the beads defines the pattern as much as does the color—experi-ment with different bead sizes and shapes. The beading glue dries to a transparent finish, and a final coat is used as a protective seal for the piece.

glass-beaded frame

Makes one frame

1 Using medium sandpaper sand the area of the frame to be beaded. Sketch your desired design on the frame with a pencil.

2 Run a line of glue along the outside edges of the front face of the frame. Hold a length of threaded seed beads tightly on both ends and lay into glue. Press beads lightly with your finger to set into glue, adjusting their position with the edge of a craft knife if necessary. When glue becomes tacky, carefully pull the thread through the beads to remove. Repeat for the inside edge of frame face. Allow glue to dry.

3 Outline the edges of the sketched design with glue. Using the same technique as in step 2, place a threaded row of mini-bugle beads along each line, remove the thread when set, and allow glue to dry.

4 Fill in the interior area of the frame by applying glue to small sections of the design and applying rows of beads, pushing threaded rows up against each other with a craft knife, and removing thread once beads have set. Fill in tight areas with single beads. When frame is finished, allow it to dry for 24 hours. Apply a light coat of the glue over the entire beaded surface and dry for one week.

VARIATION
For festive candle displays, glue rows of beads to glass votive candleholders.

MATERIALS
- finished flatface frame
- tan threaded seed beads
- black threaded mini-bugle beads
- beading glue
- general craft supplies

TIPS
Beading the edges of the frame and sketched design first creates a firm guideline for placing the remaining beads. Allow the "bead guidelines" to dry completely before proceeding with interior bead placement.

ARTIST: SANDRA SALAMONY

Revitalize thrift-shop and yard-sale finds by adding fun mosaic accents. The eclectic mix of recycled broken china and tile is unified by sanded grout, which is available in many colors or can be tinted at home (see Tips). When looking for china pieces, notice the colors and patterns that will give your piece its identity, then choose plain tile pieces to complement them. Because this project is meant for inside use, you can use thick, tacky craft glue to adhere the mosaic, a less expensive option than tile adhesive.

mosaic
candy dish

Makes one dish

1 Clean and dry dish. Make a paper template of the area to be covered. Snip tile and china pieces into irregular shapes with tile nipper, and arrange on template until area is filled.

2 Apply a layer of tacky craft glue to the tray and transfer the cut shapes onto the glue. Let dry.

3 Following the manufacturer's directions, mix sanded grout with water in a disposable container until it has a fudgelike consistency. Wearing rubber gloves, spread grout into spaces between tiles with a grout float. Let set for 10–15 minutes, then brush away excess grout with a stiff brush or an old toothbrush. Allow to dry for another 10 minutes. Wipe away remaining loose grout with a damp soft cloth or sponge, then polish tiles with a dry cloth to remove any leftover haze.

4 Apply 2–3 coats of grout sealer according to manufacturer's recommendations.

MATERIALS
- metal tray or dish
- tile and china pieces
- tile nippers
- tacky craft glue
- sanded grout
- grout float or flat-blade spreader tool
- grout sealer
- general craft supplies

VARIATION
Accent ashtrays, cake plates, flat faced frames, or trivets with mosaic patterns.

TIPS
Wear safety glasses and gloves when cutting tile with nippers. If the tray's finish is chipped, spray on two coats of metallic spray enamel or touch up finish with metallic leafing pens. Always use sanded grout rather than premixed latex grout for mosaic projects with spaces larger than 1/8" (.3 cm) between pieces. Sanded grout is available in many colors, but to save money, purchase off-white grout and add a small amount of acrylic paint, paste food color, cold-water dye, or strong tea or coffee to tint the dry grout before adding water.

ARTIST: CONNIE SHEERIN

The lovely painted pansies on this vase will rival any
blossoms you display in it, keeping the magic of wild
flowers in your home throughout the winter months.
The flowers are composed of deceptively simple single
brush strokes. Practice them on a piece of test glass to
become comfortable with this watercoloring technique.
Experiment on other glassware such as ice tea glasses or
a juice pitcher for coordinating pieces, or paint other
botanicals for variety.

painted
pansy vase

Makes one vase

1 Wash vase well with soap and water, and rinse. Dip vase in mixture of equal parts vinegar and water. Let dry.

2 To paint the pansy petals, double-load your flat brush with lavender and purple paints, lavender on one flat side and purple on the other. Press the brush flat to the glass, then quickly stroke in a heart shape. Repeat with peach and buttermilk paints.

3 Create the leaves with one stroke by pressing the brush loaded with avocado paint to the glass, curling the brush then lifting quickly. Add cadmium yellow dots with an up and down motion using the handle end of the brush.

4 Let the finished vase cure for 24 hours. Heat-set in the oven at 325°F (162°C) for 45 minutes, or according to paint manufacturer's directions.

MATERIALS

- glass vase
- ultragloss glass painting enamels in lavender, purple, peach, buttermilk, avocado, and cadmium yellow
- flat shader brush #10
- general craft supplies

VARIATION

Use this technique on glass tiles to make a unique backsplash or tiled serving tray.

TIPS

After washing vase, wear cotton gloves when handling the glass to prevent oils from your skin from marring the surface and preventing enamel from adhering. Use soft brushes to prevent colors from streaking, and wash brushes well after each use. Do not dilute paints with water—see manufacturer's instructions.

ARTIST: MARAL KACMICHIAN

metal, wire, & wood projects

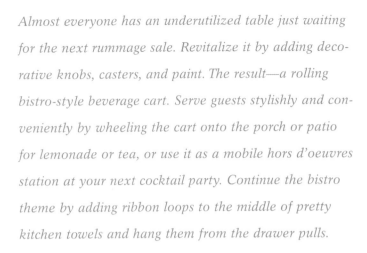

Almost everyone has an underutilized table just waiting for the next rummage sale. Revitalize it by adding decorative knobs, casters, and paint. The result—a rolling bistro-style beverage cart. Serve guests stylishly and conveniently by wheeling the cart onto the porch or patio for lemonade or tea, or use it as a mobile hors d'oeuvres station at your next cocktail party. Continue the bistro theme by adding ribbon loops to the middle of pretty kitchen towels and hang them from the drawer pulls.

bistro beverage cart

Makes one beverage cart

1 Sand the table with the wood grain and wipe off dust using a slightly damp paper towel. Paint on primer and let dry according to manufacturer's directions. Apply one coat off-white latex with foam brush. Let dry overnight. Sand lightly with fine sandpaper and remove dust. Apply a second coat off-white latex and let dry overnight.

2 Divide tabletop into five sections on the short end. With painter's tape, mask the areas that will be off-white stripes. Mask the edges and the underside of the tabletop also. Paint the exposed areas with three coats of green acrylic paint, allowing to dry 30 minutes between applications. Carefully remove tape, and touch-up off-white areas if necessary.

3 Drill starter holes for hardware: center the chrome handle on short end of table top, and evenly space holes for three drawer pulls on one long end. Install the casters on leg bottoms. Apply 2 coats of varnish to the tabletop and underside, following manufacturer's instructions. When completely dry, attach hardware.

VARIATION

Decorate the finished tabletop with stencils or rubber stamps.

MATERIALS

- Wooden table
- 1 quart latex primer
- 1 quart off-white latex, eggshell finish
- 4 ounces light-green craft acrylic paint
- 3 chrome drawer pulls
- chrome handle with visible screws
- four 1-1/4" (3.5 cm) casters
- water-based satin varnish
- general craft supplies

ARTIST: DAWN ANDERSON

Add tropical flavor to your next poolside, garden, or patio party with these special place mats made from bamboo. Their natural, wood texture lends exotic simplicity to light lunches, brunches, and tea. Use them to bring the outdoors inside on rainy days, or feel like you're on vacation anytime. A simple wrapping of wire holds the bamboo in place and allows for easy roll-up storage.

bamboo
placemats

Makes four mats

1 Saw each 43" (109 cm) bamboo cane into three 14" (36 cm) lengths for a total of 180 pieces. Vary each piece slightly for a rustic look.

2 To make the first place mat, choose a random selection of 45 canes and lay them side by side, interspersing thick and thin pieces. Cut 2 yards (1.8 m) of the cloth-covered wire and fold in half. Place the first cane in the fold of the wire about 1" (3 cm) from the end of the bamboo. Cross the wire over itself to form an X, and pull tight. Hold second cane firmly against wire crossover, and crisscross the wires in the same direction around it. Continue binding the canes together in this manner, and at the last cane twist the wire ends together, clip off the excess, and bend the twisted section to the back of the mat to hide. Bind the opposite edge using the same process, then add a second band of wire to each edge.

3 Complete the remaining place mats, following step 2.

VARIATIONS
Don't just use one color of ribbon wire. Experiment by developing a palette of coordinating hues, or by using uncovered metal wire. Instead of the natural golden bamboo featured here, try using reeds that have been dyed green. To add more bamboo accents to a table, use the same technique to make a table runner, coasters, or sleeves for glass votive candleholders.

TIP
Bamboo is very fibrous, and even sharp pruning shears may crack or split the reeds. If you don't have access to a specialized bamboo saw, try using an inexpensive disposable craftsaw blade and craft knife handle to make clean cuts when sawing.

MATERIALS
• sixty 43" (109 cm) bamboo canes
• four 10-yard (9.1 m) spools of 30-gauge cloth-covered wire
• bamboo saw (or substitute—see Tip)
• general craft supplies

ARTIST: ELIZABETH CAMERON

Delicate silver spiral drops combined with a ball chain resemble the dewy purity of a gentle spring rain. Bending sterling wire with pliers is an easy way to enter the world of custom jewelry making. The spirals should be airy and not wound too tightly; only two to three rotations of the silver wire are needed. You can also attach the spiral drops to an existing necklace to personalize a plain piece of jewelry, or make coordinating earrings for a special gift set.

falling-rain
necklace

ARTIST: KATHLEEN FREY

Makes one necklace

1 Bend one end of the sterling silver wire with the tip of round-nose pliers to start the spiral shape. Hold this partial circle flat inside the flat-nose pliers and pull the long length of wire by hand to form the next ring of the spiral, shifting the spiral in the pliers to keep the revolutions smooth. After 2–3 revolutions, bend the wire at a 45° angle using the flat nose pliers. Cut the spiral loose with wire cutters, leaving about 1" (3 cm) of straight wire. Repeat for remaining spirals. Vary the size and stem length of each spiral.

2 Lay the spirals in the order and direction you want them to hang. To prevent tangling, vary the spiral height positions, aligning spirals with straight wire sections. Beginning with the center spiral, bend the top of the straight wire section wire to a 90° angle. Cut the wire, leaving approximately 1/4" (.5 cm) past the bend. Using the tips of the round-nose pliers, bend this short wire section into a loop small enough to prevent the spiral from sliding around on the chain. Open the loop and position the spiral at the center of the chain between adjoining balls and close with flat-nose pliers. Repeat this process with all of the spirals, spacing them out evenly from the center.

3 Trim the chain to the desired length with wire cutters. Finish each end by catching one or two chain balls in a bead-tip cup and squeezing the bead tip closed with flat-nose pliers. Attach the clasp to one end and the jump ring to the other end.

TIPS

Wear protective eyewear when working with metal wire. To determine how much wire to leave for each spiral's attaching loop, create a test loop with scrap wire. When attaching the clasp to the bead tips, open and close the rings on the more flexible sterling clasp instead of on the tin bead tip.

MATERIALS

- 12" (30 cm) 24-gauge half-hard sterling silver wire
- 14" (36 cm) 1.5-mm sterling silver ball chain
- 2 side-closing bead tips
- 1 sterling clasp with jump ring
- round-nose and flat-nose pliers
- wire cutters

ARTIST: MARTHA THURLOW

What could be simpler and yet more personal than this frame that becomes part of the art with just stamps, ink, and sealer? Create a unique presentation for your photographs and other images by letting the framed image inspire you—apply coordinating accents, design random or repeating patterns, or use letter stamps to personalize the frames with names or other words. Children will enjoy making this fun and easy project.

stamped
picture frame

Makes one frame

1 Remove the glass from the frame. Stamp the frame in the desired design with the stamping paint. Let dry.

2 Over a protected surface, apply the spray varnish according to manufacturer's directions. Let dry thoroughly.

3 Reassemble the frame.

VARIATIONS

Customize your frame even further by carving your own stamps with materials purchased at craft stores. Use embossing powder to add dimension to the stamped images. Stain or paint the frame first for other colorful options.

MATERIALS
- wooden frame
- stamps
- acrylic stamping ink
- spray acrylic varnish
- general craft supplies

Harmonious layers of sponged and stamped paper add depth to this playful clock. Create color combinations to suit the decor in all rooms of your house, from a child's bedroom to the kitchen. Experiment with printed papers such as book pages, old menus, and sheet music. If you don't have tools available to cut the clock form to your desired shape, purchase a clock kit that includes a precut clock form and the clockworks.

layered-paper
wall clock

Makes one clock

1 Cut wood to desired size and shape for clock form. Drill a hole where clockworks shaft will fit.

2 Trim the first layer of paper slightly larger than the clock form. Brush PVA glue on the back of the paper and press firmly to clock form, smoothing away any air bubbles. Fold overhanging paper around sides to cover edges, keeping corners neat.

3 Sponge, rubber stamp, and emboss your desired patterns on two contrasting sheets of paper. Cut one sheet slightly smaller than clock form, and cut the second sheet just smaller than first piece.

4 Stamp and emboss the clock face with either a single dial stamp or individual numbered stamps on another sheet of decorative paper. Cut out face in a circle. Cut a larger circle and stripe the edge with colored markers.

5 Glue the layers of paper to the clock form, from largest to smallest, being careful to center clock face circles over the pre-drilled hole for the clockworks. Poke a hole through all of the layers through the pre-drilled opening and assemble the clockworks to finish.

VARIATION
In addition to decorating the clock with stamps, consider gluing on pressed flowers and leaves.

MATERIALS
- wood for clock form
- clockworks
- PVA glue
- decorative papers as desired
- rubber stamps and ink
- colored markers
- embossing powder
- heat embossing tool
- general craft supplies

ARTIST: MARTHA THURLOW

Create twisted wire balls, wrapped beads, and simple beads with wire loops and assemble them into this delicate yet strong choker necklace. Steel wire links the beads together and is twisted to fashion a simple hook and ring closure. Choose vintage glass beads in interesting shapes and colors to complement the earthy tone of the steel. Create a matching bracelet to make a gift set.

wirework
bead necklace

Makes one choker-length necklace

1 To make a wire ball, cut a length of wire about 12" (30 cm) long and make a loop at one end. About 1/4" (.5 cm) below the loop, bend the wire back on itself. Hold the doubled wire secure with flat-nose pliers and manipulate wire by hand around the doubled section, wrapping the wire as if winding a ball of string to form a wire bead form. When the ball is the desired size, thread the wire end through the center and form a loop on the opposite end of the first loop. Repeat to make additional beads.

2 Wire-wrap each long bead by cutting an 8" (20 cm) length of wire. Bend the wire at a 90° angle 2" (5 cm) from one end. Turn long end in a loop at the bend with round nose pliers, returning wire to 90° position. Hold loop firmly with flat-nose pliers and wrap long wire section once around the 2" (5 cm) post just above the loop. Slide a bead on the short section of wire and hold firmly against wire twist. Wrap the long section of the wire around the bead 1–2 times and then around the center post at the end of the bead. Cut away excess wrapping wire and squeeze the end flat with the flat-nose wires to prevent scratches. Bend the center wire to a 90° angle, trim to about 3/8" (1 cm), and create a loop with the round-nose pliers. Repeat on as many beads as necessary for your necklace.

3 The round beads only need loops on either end. Working with a comfortable length of wire, create a loop on one end by bending about 3/8" (1 cm) at a right angle with the flat-nose pliers. Use the round-nose pliers to form the loop. Slide the bead onto the wire so it rests against the loop. Bend the wire at a 90° angle tightly against the bead, trim the wire to 3/8", and create a loop with the round-nose pliers.

4 Arrange completed beads in a 14" to16" (36 cm to 41 cm) string. Link beads together by opening and closing the loops by twisting wire sideways with flat-nose pliers rather than unwinding loops. Remember that one of the loops on each wire-wrapped bead cannot be opened.

5 Create a clasp by cutting a 6" (15 cm) length of wire for the hook. Bend it in half tightly with flat-nose pliers and fashion a 1/2" (1 cm) long rounded hook shape at the fold. Grasp the wire tails 3/4" (2 cm) from the hook with flat-nose pliers; bend one tail at a 90° angle forward and the other at a 90° angle backward. Using one of the tails, wrap down the two hook wires to form a tight coil, holding the wire pair together with the flat-nose pliers while wrapping. Trim away any excess wire. Trim the remaining tail to 1/2" (1 cm) and create a loop with round-nose pliers. Attach to one end of necklace at loop. To create the hook's ring, wrap a 2" (5 cm) length of wire around the base of the round-nose pliers to create a circle. Remove any excess wire, tighten the ring with the flat-nose pliers, and add to the end of the necklace to complete.

MATERIALS

- 22-gauge steel wire
- long opaque glass beads
- round translucent beads
- round-nose and flat-nose pliers
- wire cutters
- general craft supplies

TIP

Wear protective eyewear when working with wire.

Similar to inlay in appearance, marquetry consists of trimmed wood veneer shapes that cover an entire surface with no inlaid pieces. The technique shown here is properly called parquetry because the shapes are all geometric like a parquet floor. This method utilizes pressure-sensitive wood veneer that is easy to cut and adhere; a square frame simplifies pattern making. Traditional marquetry achieves color contrast only through differing wood varieties, but you can also stain selected woods prior to cutting if desired.

marquetry
wood-veneer frame

Makes one frame

1 If unfinished, stain frame to desired tone. Let dry. Sand area to be veneered with fine sandpaper and remove dust with a damp paper towel. Stain one strip of wood veneer to chosen color if desired; let dry.

2 Using cut pieces of scrap paper, a triangle, and a ruler, develop a pattern to fit the frame using simple, repeating geometric shapes. Create a stencil for the basic pieces from scrap cardboard. Lightly sketch the outline of the stencil on the desired wood strips and cut the veneer into shaped pieces with scissors. Cut edging strips and miter corners.

3 Remove paper backing from veneer pieces and press firmly into place following manufacturer's directions. Place veneer pieces as close to each other as possible, trimming when necessary. With a burnisher or brayer, roll over the placed veneer pieces with firm, even pressure to secure.

4 Finish entire piece with two coats of water-based varnish, allowing it to dry between applications.

VARIATIONS

Create a marquetry mat from veneer scraps to provide an interesting background for the framed artwork. This technique can also liven up serving trays and wooden shelf edges.

MATERIALS

- square flat-faced frame
- pressure-sensitive veneer strips in contrasting woods
- water-based colored stain (optional)
- burnisher or brayer
- water-based satin varnish
- general craft supplies

TIPS

To create a template for a square frame, begin by drawing a rectangle the size of one face edge of the frame, minus one corner squared, and subtract the area that the edging strips will fill. This template will serve for all sides of the frame. The wood veneers may look dull at first, but the finishing varnish will bring out the rich wood grain.

ARTIST: SANDRA SALAMONY

This versatile serving tray has the treasured look of a piece that's been handed down for generations, providing a graceful way to present drinks or food to your guests. Choose your decorative images from wallpaper, gift wrap, greeting cards, and magazines; if you wish, adorn the sides of the tray, too. Create coordinating coasters for a matched serving set (see page 44 for a technique for making coasters).

floral
decoupage tray

Makes one tray

1 Sand tray lightly with fine sandpaper and remove dust with a slightly misted paper towel. Brush two coats of acrylic paint on the wooden tray with a foam brush, allowing tray to dry between applications. Let dry.

2 Cut images from gift wrap, wallpaper, cards, magazines, or color-copied reproductions with small, sharp scissors or craft knife and cutting mat. Trim China bristle brush to a diagonal edge.

3 With a foam brush, apply a thin coat of decoupage medium to the area of the tray where the images will be placed. Place trimmed images firmly on the tray, and burnish with the trimmed China bristle brush to remove extra medium and air bubbles. Let dry for one hour.

4 Paint the edges of the tray with gold metallic acrylic paint and let dry. Apply two to three thin coats of water-based varnish with a foam brush to entire tray, allowing it to dry between applications.

MATERIALS

- unfinished wooden tray
- acrylic paint for base color
- printed images
- decoupage medium
- China bristle brush
- metallic gold acrylic paint
- water-based satin varnish
- general craft supplies

VARIATIONS

To further enhance the vintage look of the piece, apply a layer of a transparent crackle medium after the decoupage medium has completely dried. Rub burnt umber acrylic paint lightly into the crackled surface to simulate aging. To protect the tray from spilled drinks, have a glass store cut a thin piece of sheet acrylic to fit inside your tray.

ARTIST: SUE HANDMAN

Whether you're framing three vacation photos, three pictures of children, or three generations of wedding portraits, this solid cherry triptych frame presents them with style. Danish oil brings out the color and detail of the wood grain while protecting its surface, and brass darkening solution applied to bright brass nails creates a weathered appearance that complements the finish of the hinges. The edges of the wood need not be cut perfectly—let the rough-sawn edges of the cherry plank add to the distinctive appearance of this frame.

hinged
triptych frame

Makes one frame

1 Saw the cherry plank into three 6" (15 cm) wide panels and sand edges smooth. Wipe away sawdust with a lightly misted paper towel or a tack cloth. Apply Danish oil with a soft cloth, let penetrate 5 minutes, then wipe off excess according to manufacturer's directions. Repeat after 24 hours. Let dry an additional 24 hours.

2 Lay the three wood panels flat with wood grain matching. Cut a 4" x 6" (10 cm x 15 cm) template from scrap cardboard and mark three edges in 1" (3 cm) increments, omitting one short end for the top opening. Position the template at the center of one panel and mark 17 dots on the wood with a pencil at template marks and corners. Repeat to mark remaining panels. Center hinge over each join, separating the panels enough to clear the hinge pin. Mark and drill starter holes for the hinge screws.

3 Following manufacturer's directions, pour brass darkening solution into a disposable glass jar and submerge the brass pins. When desired tint is achieved, remove the pins from the solution. Rinse immediately with water, and pat dry with a paper towel.

4 Hammer the brass pins partially into the wood panels at each marked dot, leaving enough space between pinhead and wood for glass pane and image. Screw hinges in place, and finish by sliding photos and glass into the "U" created by the nails.

VARIATIONS
Use weathered wood and salvaged hinges for a distressed frame.

MATERIALS

- 7 1/2" x 18" x 3/4" (19 cm x 46 cm x 2 cm) cherry plank
- three 4" x 6" (10 cm x 15 cm) pieces of picture glass
- two 2 1/2" x 2" (6 cm x 5 cm) mission-style hinges
- 51 brass escutcheon pins
- Danish oil
- brass darkening solution
- general craft supplies

TIP

If power tools are not available to cut the cherry plank, have your wood supplier saw the pieces at the time of purchase. If the darkened brass finish of the nail head is partially chipped away when hammering, apply a dab of darkening solution with a cotton swab and wipe away with the water-dampened tip of another swab.

ARTIST: SANDRA SALAMONY

Used as garden luminaries, these wire and paper candleholders add a subtle glow to evenings on the patio. The hardware cloth frame is silhouetted against the paper by the candlelight, creating a luminous yet structured effect. Hardware cloth is an inexpensive galvanized steel mesh available at most hardware stores. These holders are the perfect size to hold tea candles, but experiment with other sizes and shapes to create an eclectic mix of light. You can also vary the paper—try white rice paper for a Japanese theme.

wire-mesh votives

Makes four triangle votives

1 Wearing protective gloves, cut one rectangle of 14 x 43 squares (3 1/2" x 10 3/4") from hardware cloth with wire cutters. Clip away the wire that forms one short end to leave bare prongs.

2 Bend the rectangle in thirds to create a triangular form with faces of 14 squares (3 1/2" square, or 9 cm square). Attach the short ends by looping the bare wire prongs of one end around the other, adjoining ends, and pinch them closed with pliers.

3 Cut a 3 1/2" x 11 1/2" (9 cm x 29 cm) rectangle from the paper. Mix 2 parts matte medium with 1 part water in a container. Wrap the paper around the wire form and paint thickly with matte medium mixture. Soak the paper thoroughly with the mixture, pressing it firmly to the wire form with the foam brush to adhere. Overlap the paper at short ends and press to seal. Let dry.

MATERIALS
- handmade papers, assorted colors
- 1 roll 1/4" (.5 cm) weave hardware cloth
- acrylic matte medium
- general craft supplies

TIP
Tea candles come with metal containers; use a clear glass candle base for other sized candles.

ARTIST: SANDRA SALAMONY

Add flare to plain candlesticks with these embossed metal collars. The completed design fits around standard sized tapers, but you can enlarge the supplied pattern to make collars for candles of other sizes. Dress up your dining table for parties or the holidays with a group of metal flowers, and change the colors of the beads to match your décor. Combine with wire and bead napkin rings (page 159) for a coordinated table setting.

embossed brass
candle collar

ARTIST: KELLEY TAYLOR

Makes one candle collar

1 Photocopy pattern from page 168 at 150%. Place metal on several newspapers or a magazine to protect working surface, and tape down corners. Tape the copied patterns to the metal. Using an awl, trace over the pattern lines to transfer image to the foil. Punch holes in pattern (A) piece as indicated, with a hammer and awl. Remove patterns; cut out designs.

2 Press and drag awl to make leaf vein impressions on the metal. Gently bend each leaf to curl edges up. Hot glue the bottom of piece (A) to the top of piece (B).

3 Cut eight 3" (8 cm) lengths of beading wire. Bend one end of each wire into a loop for hanging. Thread desired beads onto wire, then curl the end of the wire around the awl 3–4 times to secure beads in place. Trim excess wire. Hang the beaded wire pieces from the holes in piece (A).

VARIATIONS
Brush the metal surface with steel wool for a matte finish. Use other toned foils for this project such as copper or aluminum.

TIPS
To cut center holes, punch several times in the middle with an awl to provide an opening for scissors. Wear protective gloves when working with metal as edges are sharp.

MATERIALS
- lightweight brass embossing metal or tooling foil
- templates (A) and (B) (page 168)
- brass beading wire
- beads
- awl
- general craft supplies

ARTIST: CATHY R. MCLAURIN

Here's a whimsical decorative box that's useful for storing keys, jewelry, or small treasures. This easy decoupage technique uses white craft glue and water-based varnish to seal the images. Decorate the container with a collage of themed images and cutout text, or try an eclectic mix of similar hues. Begin with an unfinished box and paint or stain it to coordinate with your chosen images, or revitalize and recycle an old box. Line the box with colorful fibrous paper to protect and finish the inside.

decoupage collage
keepsake box

Makes one box

1 Sand wooden box lightly with fine sandpaper. Wipe away dust with a slightly misted paper towel.

2 Cut images from old books, magazines, or color-copied reproductions with small, sharp scissors or a craft knife and cutting mat. Trim decorative paper to desired size. Spread white craft glue onto the back of each cutout image and paper with a foam brush and apply to desired area of the box. Rub images with a soft, dry cloth to press out any air bubbles or excess glue. Remove any excess glue with a slightly damp sponge. Allow to dry.

3 Apply six coats of water-based satin varnish with a foam brush, brushing each coat in alternating directions, allowing to dry thoroughly between coats. When final coat of varnish has completely dried, lightly rub the box with fine steel wool.

VARIATION

Liven up other pieces of wooden furniture, such as chair backs, CD cabinets, and coffee tables with decoupaged images.

TIP

To smooth air bubbles and remove excess glue from placed prints easily, place a sheet of wax paper over the image and rub gently with a bone folder.

MATERIALS
- wooden box
- printed images
- decorative paper
- white craft glue
- bone folder (optional)
- water-based satin varnish
- general craft supplies

Ornamental and festive, this candleholder is made from copper foil that is thin enough to be cut with just a pair of scissors or easily embossed or pierced. The base of each candleholder is made from the circular bottom of a recycled aluminum soda can. Create multiple holders to hold groups of candles of varying heights for a dramatic centerpiece for your dinner table. For variety, make this project with other tinted metal foils such as tin.

copper candleholders

Makes one candleholder

1 Photocopy the template from page 170. Using scissors, cut a piece of copper foil 1" (3 cm) longer than the template. Tape the foil flat over a newspaper or magazine to provide a soft work surface. Tape the template over the copper and transfer the design to the metal by tracing over the lines with a ballpoint pen.

2 Cut out the perimeter of the design with scissors. Using an awl, pierce a series of holes following the interior embossed lines. Create another series of holes along the top edge of the foil if desired. Hold a ruler along the dotted fold line on the left side of the foil piece. Fold the thin edge of foil to the left of the line up and over to the center of the piece. Turn foil over and repeat for the dotted line on the right side. Interlink these folds on the short ends to form a cylinder of the foil and press to close.

3 Wearing a pair of protective gloves, pierce the aluminum soda can near the top with a pair of scissors. Cut down to the base of the can, and cut around base to separate the circular bottom.

4 Cut the series of tabs along the bottom of the project as marked on the template. Insert the upturned circular section from the soda can into the foil cylinder. Turn the tabs inside to hold the circular base in position, and apply two or three drops of super glue to secure the can section.

VARIATION
It's easy to create an aged and darkened finish on the copper: wearing rubber gloves, wipe the finished piece with a weak solution of liver of sulfur and water according to package directions, then brush with steel wool to polish.

MATERIALS
- 12" x 4" (30 cm x 10 cm) strip copper foil
- template (see page 170)
- awl
- aluminum soda can
- super glue
- general craft supplies

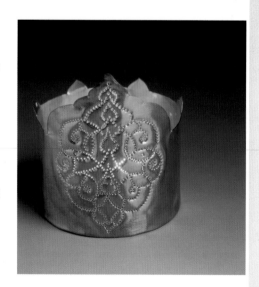

TIP
A large needle can be substituted for the awl.

ARTIST: MICHAEL BALL

Aluminum cans are recycled into art in this layered wall hanging. Follow the supplied template to create embossed leaf patterns in the metal and mount the leaves on layers of decorative papers embellished with metallic paint. Wire and bead accents complete the hanging, which is held together by jump rings and rivets. Use coordinating papers that complement your decorating scheme, or make different wall hangings for each season to display in your entryway.

mixed-media
wall hanging

Makes one wall hanging

1 Cut or tear the papers in decreasing sizes. Highlight the corrugated paper with gold paint and a piece of scrap fabric. Stamp the front piece of paper with ink and crumpled plastic wrap, then emboss with clear embossing powder and a heat embossing gun while ink is still wet. Embellish paper as desired with silver pen.

2 Cut open aluminum soda can and discard ends. Photocopy design from page 169 at 150%. Tape copy paper to printed side of cans. On a soft surface such as a magazine, trace the design with a stylus or ballpoint pen to emboss the metal. Cut out the design. Repeat as desired.

3 Bend wire into freehand shapes, hammer flat where desired, and embellish with beads.

4 Assemble the papers and wire shapes; secure with spray adhesive. Attach the aluminum leaves to the top with double-stick foam. Using rivet pliers, attach the sections together with rivets and jump rings.

VARIATION
Alter the color palette and aluminum design for a wall decoration with a holiday or seasonal theme.

MATERIALS
- colored paper
- handmade paper
- corrugated cardboard
- aluminum soda cans
- template (page 169)
- 20-gauge wire
- beads
- jump rings
- rivets
- rivet plier
- metallic gold acrylic paint
- heat embossing gun
- embossing powder and ink
- metallic silver pen
- spray adhesive
- double-stick foam
- general craft supplies

TIPS
Wear protective gloves when cutting aluminum cans. Place the layers in order with aluminum on top before gluing to check sizes and placement.

ARTIST: CHRISTINE BAKHOLDIN

Indulge a flight of fancy with these whimsical and wearable

works of art. Whether you create clever animal designs, stylish

swirls, or geometric symbols, these attractive pins add personality

to any outfit. Customize these pins as gifts, or make two of the

same design for friendship jewelry. You can also experiment with

the texture of the metal by hammering curves for additional

interest and to harden the wire.

sculpted
steel pins

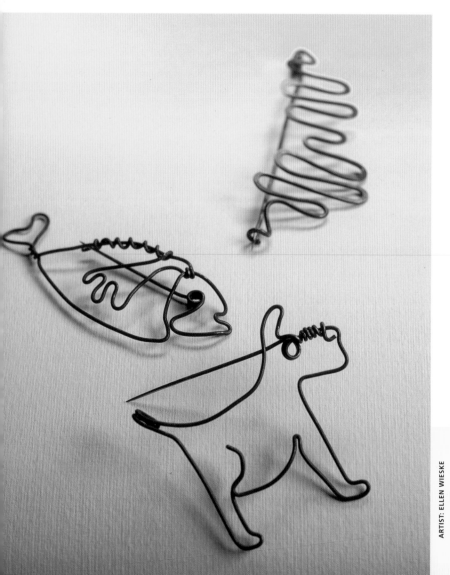

Makes one pin

1 Draw the designs on paper first to plan the bends and curves of the single length of steel wire, or follow the diagrams on page 168. Then secure the wire in a vise 4" (10 cm) from one end. Holding the short end in vise grips, twist the 4" (10 cm) section until very stiff, forming the pin stem.

2 Immediately after the pin stem, turn wire into two small loops with round-nose pliers to make a spring.

3 Shape remaining wire into pin form, using the pliers to hold and bend the metal. Follow a drawn pattern, or create free-form designs. Hammer the metal in selected spots as desired.

4 Fashion a hook from the end of the wire to hold the pin stem. Trim and sharpen pin stem end with nail file or sandpaper.

MATERIALS

• 24" (61 cm) 18-gauge annealed steel wire
• vise and vise grips
• round-nose pliers
• general craft supplies

TIP

To avoid uncomfortable sharp ends, pin stem should not be excessively longer than the hook end.

ARTIST: ELLEN WIESKE

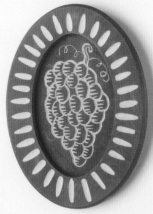

These bold and unique kitchen wall plaques are a perfect introduction to the art of woodcarving. The striking style of the carved images is very forgiving of small errors, and is enhanced by the bright finish of the dyed wood. Using cold-water fabric dye instead of stain creates an intense yet transparent wash of color that allows the wood grain to show. Basswood is softer than many other woods, providing a versatile canvas for the novice carver.

ARTIST: CINDY GORDER

carved
wood plaques

Makes one tray

1 Sand tray if necessary, and remove dust. Mix package of powdered dye with 1 cup warm water. Stir until completely dissolved. With a foam brush, apply the dye liberally to all surfaces of the wooden plaque. Let dry one hour.

2 Enlarge pattern from page 169 by 200%, and then trace it onto tracing paper. Attach pattern to dry plaque with low-tack masking tape. Insert white transfer paper, coated side down, in between the wood and pattern. Follow the pattern lines with a pencil to transfer the image to the plaque.

3 With the V-parting tool, make the outline cuts of the design by holding the tool at a slight angle to the wood surface and pushing it with light pressure, removing only small amounts of wood at each stroke. Always carve in the direction away from you. Fill in shading lines with the same tool. Use the straight gouge carving tool to create wider lines for the border if desired.

4 Center and attach a sawtooth picture hanger to the back of the plaque.

VARIATIONS
Treat the finished plaque with a food-safe finish to create a tray. Once you've mastered wood carving on a relatively flat surface, graduate to other unfinished basswood products such as boxes or frames for additional decorating options.

MATERIALS
- unfinished basswood tray
- cold-water fabric dyes in desired colors
- bent V-parting carving tool
- straight gouge carving tool
- small sawtooth picture hanger
- pattern (see page 169)
- general craft supplies

TIPS
Apply two or more coats of dye to darken the color. Mix dyes to create unique hues for your project. For the cleanest cuts, carve with the grain of the wood. Initial cuts can be widened by tilting the carving tool to its side and re-cutting the wood inside the lines.

A plain wooden bowl comes alive with freehand applications of paint and glaze, a perfect way to recycle an old bowl, or decorate a newly purchased piece. The finished bowl creates a lovely display, either featured alone or with a fruit arrangement, and makes a charming housewarming gift. Create one special bowl design, or paint an eclectic group of different-size bowls for a table centerpiece. Surface preparation is the key to success, as well as careful, patient attention to varnishing steps.

painted
french-twist bowl

Makes one bowl

1 Sand bowl with medium sandpaper and remove dust. Seal bowl with two coats of water-based primer, sanding with fine sandpaper between coats; let dry. Apply two layers of darker acrylic base coat with a foam brush. When dry, apply two coats of water-based gloss varnish, sanding with fine sandpaper between coats. Let dry.

2 Transfer the design from page 169 to the bowl, or draw a freehand design of your own. Paint design with small synthetic brushes and the complementary shade of acrylic paint. When dry, apply another coat of varnish. Let dry thoroughly.

3 Mix glaze with the lighter shade of acrylic base coat, and apply evenly to entire bowl surface. Create designs in the glaze by removing paint in patterns with the rubber combing tool. Let dry, then apply another two coats of varnish.

4 Create a smooth final surface by applying several additional coats of varnish, gently wet-sanding between coats after drying with fine sandpaper that has been dampened with soap and water.

MATERIALS

- wooden bowl
- water-based primer
- water-based gloss varnish
- acrylic paints in two shades of base coat and one complementary color
- glazing liquid
- small rubber combing tool
- flat and script synthetic brushes
- template (page 169)
- general craft supplies

TIP

In addition to using a rubber combing tool to create patterns in the glaze, experiment with a Color Shaper® or rubber-tip tool. Use a hairdryer between coats of paint and varnish to accelerate drying time. Be sure to finish the outside of the bowl to seal.

ARTIST: JUDITH G. MILLER

Make your home sparkle with these delightful candles. Covering inexpensive pillar candles with microglitter is a fast way to add a festive touch to any occasion. Experiment with coordinating color palates, vertical or horizontal stripes, and patterns to personalize these twinkling pillars that are perfect for gifts, for elaborate table settings, or to add unexpected sparkle to a quiet corner of your home. Vary the candle sizes for sophisticated groupings, and sprinkle some leftover glitter on the candle stands to reflect even more of the flames' glow.

glitter-encrusted candles

Makes two candles

1 On a sheet of craft paper, sprinkle a generous amount of each color of glitter in three bands. Brush glitter lightly to blend colors. When desired effect is achieved, shift paper gently back and forth to spread glitter evenly.

2 Wipe the candle with rubbing alcohol to clean. Apply a coat of candle painting medium with a foam brush.

3 Roll the candle across the glitter, holding at the top and bottom only. Let dry thoroughly. If necessary, apply additional medium and roll in the glitter again. When completely dry, tap candle to remove excess glitter. Repeat for remaining candles.

VARIATION
Glue or pin metal charms to the candles for a distinctive gift.

MATERIALS
- 2 off-white pillar candles
- candle-painting medium
- microglitter in baby blue, pastel green, and champagne
- general craft supplies

ARTIST: LIVIA MCREE

Delicate eggshells create striking mosaics when tinted with liquid watercolors, offering a unique and inexpensive way to update a flat frame. Pieces of dyed eggshell are carefully placed on the finished frame and are cracked even smaller by hand into a mosaic. Collage glue will dry clear, letting the painted frame "grout" show through and minimizing color bleed from the tinted eggs.

eggshell
mosaic frame

ARTIST: LIVIA MCREE

Makes one frame

1 Crack the eggs in half and reserve the insides for later use. Rinse shells and let dry completely. Paint eggshells with liquid watercolor paint, and spatter with accent colors if desired. When dry, spray the eggs with the fixative and let dry.

2 Paint the frame with white acrylic paint; let dry. Brush a layer of collage glue on the front surface of the frame. Break off a 1" (3 cm) square piece of colored eggshell and press it flat to the frame with your thumb until it cracks into smaller pieces. Separate the pieces apart slightly with craft knife to create mosaic. Continue in this manner until the entire frame is covered with the eggshell mosaic. If pieces of the eggshell extend past the frame edge, turn the frame over on a cutting mat and trim off excess shell with a craft knife.

3 Cover the entire frame with a coat of acrylic fixative and let dry completely.

VARIATIONS

Experiment with other pigments and decorative painting techniques when coloring the shells—try gold metallic paint or fabric dyes, and sponging or crackle finishes. Or, use naturally colored brown or speckled eggs for a simple, pure tone.

TIPS

To spatter another color on top of the base color of the eggs, let the base coat dry completely. Using a dry toothbrush lightly dipped in a contrasting watercolor, gently rub your thumb along the toothbrush to release color in a light spray of pigment. We left the membrane on the eggshell to help prevent the watercolor pigment from bleeding, but if you use other paints to color the shells remove the membrane from the eggshells after breaking.

MATERIALS
- one frame
- one dozen eggs
- liquid watercolor paints
- white acrylic paint
- spray acrylic watercolor fixative
- collage glue
- general craft supplies

ARTIST: C. D. CARTWRIGHT

Colorful beads and randomly looped wire create a playful yet sophisticated mood when fashioned into these napkin rings. Beads, buttons, and charms combine to match your dishes, place mats, and tableware season by season. Choose a random selection of vintage beads, or unify the design with similar beads of different colors. Add stamped napkins (page 78) or salt-dyed napkins (page 66) for a thoughtful housewarming gift.

wire and bead
napkin rings

Makes four napkin rings

1 Cut one yard (.9 m) of wire and turn a loop at one end with round-nose pliers. Thread a bead to the looped end, then create more loops with the pliers to hold the bead in place.

2 Continue adding beads and looping wire until beaded length is approximately 8" (20 cm). Run straight wire end through looped end to form a circle from embellished wire. Continue looping straight wire, following napkin ring circle and adding beads where desired. Wrap wire end around napkin ring when finished, hiding wire end inside a bead if possible. Repeat for remaining napkin rings.

MATERIALS

- 4 yards (3.7 m) 20- or 24-gauge craft wire
- round-nose pliers
- wire cutters
- beads, buttons, and charms
- general craft supplies

Whimsical and unique, this embellished cowbell will be the perfect accent to your patio or garden. This mosaic is created from preshaped decorative tile pieces, available from craft distributors; or you can use stones, charms, or pieces of broken tile, china, or mirror. Because the area to be tiled is three-dimensional, work one face at a time, moving to the next section only when the previous surface is dry.

mosaic
chime

Makes one chime

1 Make a paper template of one side of the cowbell. Snip tile and china pieces into irregular shapes with tile nippers or use pre-shaped mosaic pieces, and place on template until area is filled. Apply tile adhesive with a v-notch trowel or flat-blade spreader to one face of the chime and transfer the cut tile and china pieces onto the tile adhesive. Let dry. Repeat for remaining sides, leaving joins uncovered.

2 Following manufacturer's directions, mix sanded grout with water in a disposable container until it has a fudgelike consistency. Wearing rubber gloves, spread grout into spaces between tiles with a grout float. Let set for 10–15 minutes, then brush away excess grout with a stiff brush such as an old toothbrush. Allow to dry for another 10 minutes. Wipe away remaining loose grout with a damp soft cloth or sponge, then polish tiles with a dry cloth to remove any leftover haze. Repeat for remaining sides.

3 Apply 2–3 coats of grout sealer according to manufacturer's recommendations.

MATERIALS
- metal cowbell
- tile and china pieces
- tile nippers
- tile adhesive
- v-notch trowel or glue spreader
- sanded grout
- grout float or flat-blade spreader tool
- grout sealer
- general craft supplies

TIP
Wear safety glasses and gloves when cutting tile with nippers.

ARTIST: CONNIE SHEERIN

patterns

REFER TO PAGE 9
FOR TIPS ON HOW
TO TRANSFER
PATTERNS TO
YOUR PROJECTS.

A

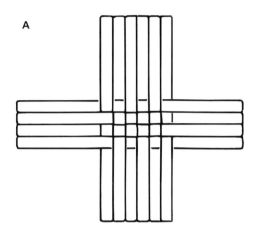

B

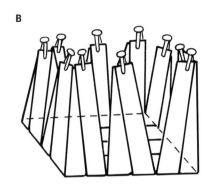

C

D

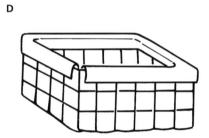

FULL VIEW

Use an image with proportions that fit your shade, approximately three units long by one unit wide.

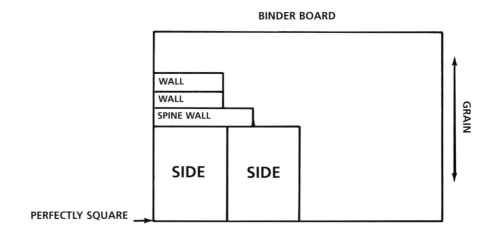

BLEACHED VELVET PILLOWS (PAGE 84)
PHOTOCOPY AT 200% OR TO FIT DESIRED SIZE.

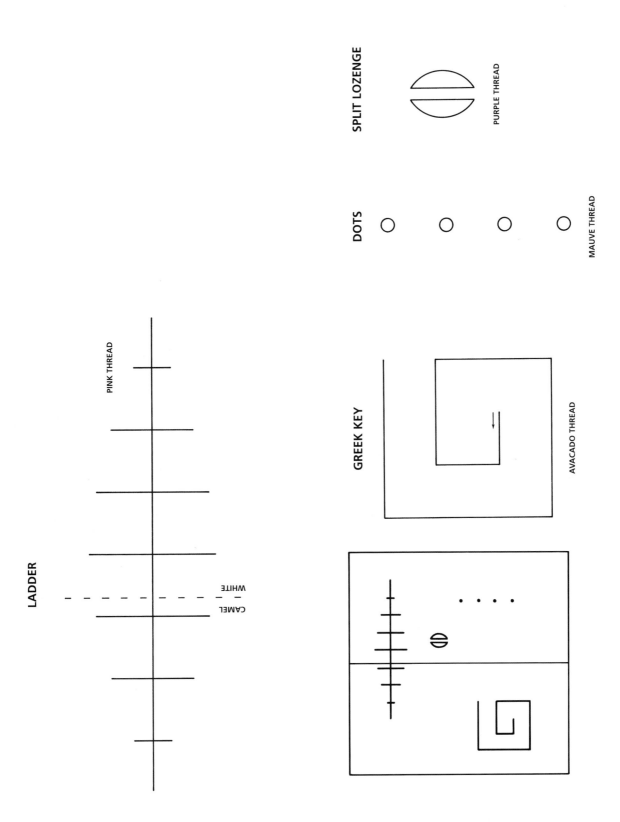

SPLIT LOZENGE

PURPLE THREAD

DOTS

MAUVE THREAD

LADDER

PINK THREAD

WHITE

CAMEL

GREEK KEY

AVACADO THREAD

LINEN DISPLAY FRAME (PAGE 83)
PHOTOCOPY AT 200%

NICHE TEMPLATE

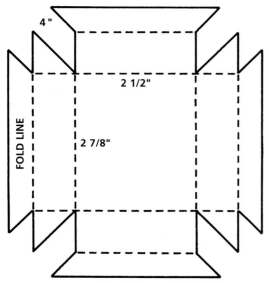

4"

FOLD LINE

2 1/2"

2 7/8"

LAYOUT GUIDE

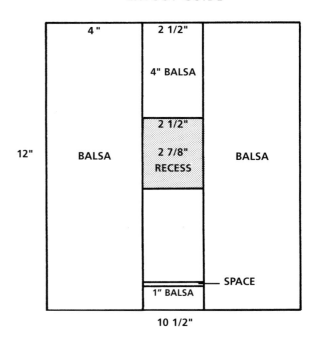

4"

2 1/2"

4" BALSA

12"

BALSA

2 1/2"

2 7/8"
RECESS

BALSA

SPACE

1" BALSA

10 1/2"

ENGRAVED SLATE FRAME (PAGE 116)
PHOTOCOPY AT 150% OR SIZE TO FIT.

KEY
R=RED
B=BLUE
G=GREEN
Y=YELLOW

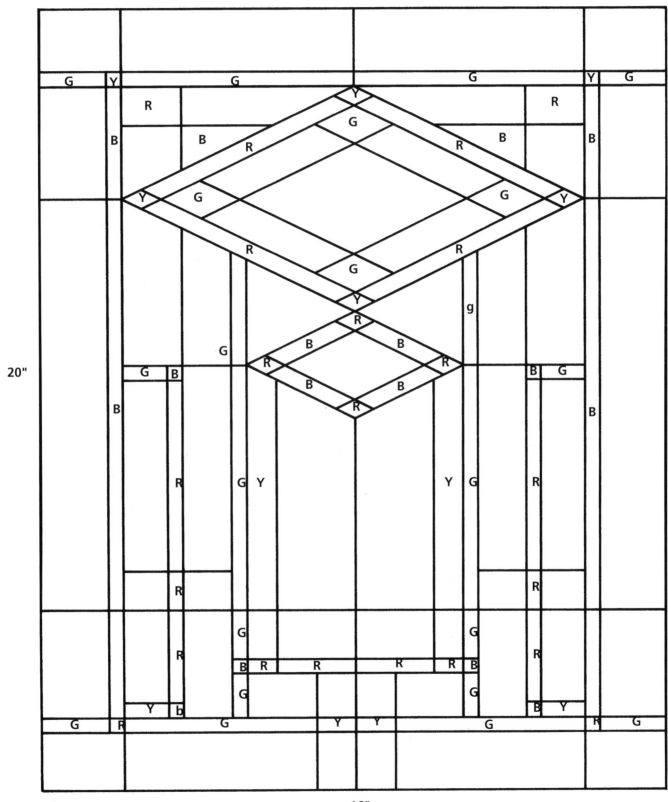

20"

16"

BRASS CANDLE COLLARS (PAGE 146)
PHOTOCOPY AT 150%.

A

B

SCULPTED STEEL PINS (PAGE 152)
PHOTOCOPY AT 150%

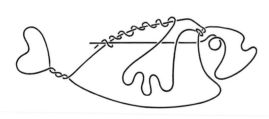

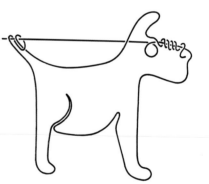

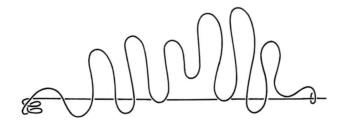

PAINTED FRENCH-TWIST BOWL (PAGE 155)
PHOTOCOPY AT 150% OR TO FIT DESIRED SIZE.

CARVED WOOD PLAQUES (PAGE 153)
PHOTOCOPY AT 200%.

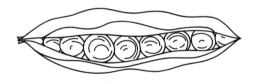

MIXED-MEDIA WALL HANGING (PAGE 151)
PHOTOCOPY AT 150%.

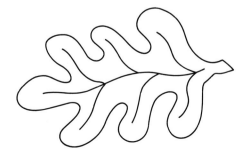

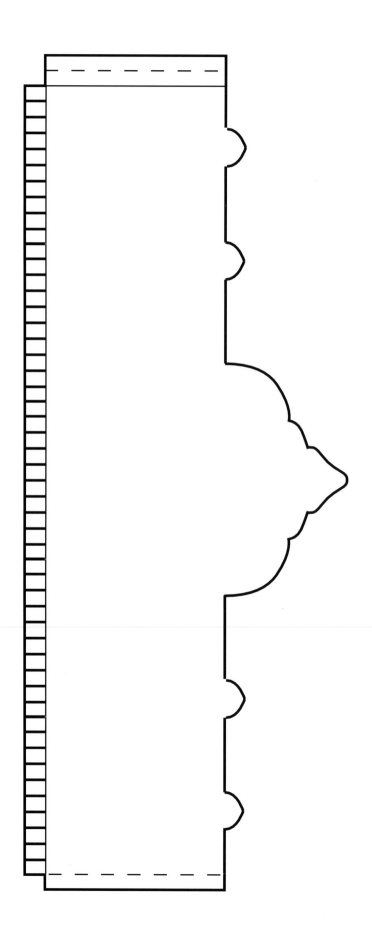

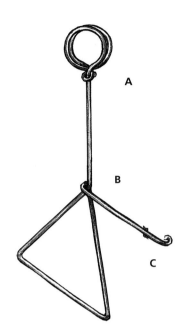

A

B

C

resources

A.C. Moore
See www.acmoore.com for store locations
art and craft supplies

Blueprints-Printables
1400-A Marsten Road
Burlingame, CA 94010-2422
phone: 1-800-356-0445
light-sensitive fabrics, p. 87

C.M. Offray & Son, Inc.
Customer Service
phone: 1-800-344-5533
ribbons, pp. 70, 88

Cape Cod Cooperage
phone: 508-432-0788
slate frames and plaques, p. 116

Crafts a la Cart
P.O. Box 246
Lansdowne, PA 19050
phone: 610-394-0992
concraft@aol.com
www.craftsalacart.com
*imported mosaic tiles and related supplies, beads, glass
etching products, pp. 120, 123, 160*

Craftopia.com
www.craftopia.com
art and craft supplies

Crafty Angels
c/o Lynda Miller
P.O. Box 3411
Thousand Oaks, CA 91359
phone: 805-373-6643
fax: 805-379-8753
www.printgocco.com/
print Gocco machine, p. 42

Daniel Smith
P.O. Box 84268
Seattle, WA 98124-5568 USA
phone: 1-800-426-6740
*artist's materials, archival papers, linoleum cutters,
Safety-Kut soft
carving block, p. 78*

Dover Publications
31 East 2nd Street
Mineola, NY 11501
phone: 516-294-7000
copyright-free images, p. 76

Dritz Fabric dyes
Prym-Dritz Corporation
Customer Service
phone: 1-800-255-7796
cold-water fabric dyes, p. 153

Fiskars, Inc.
Educational Resources Department
P.O. Box 8027
Wausau, WI 54402
www.fiskars.com
decorative-edged scissors, circle cutter, p. 16

Good Ideas
P.O. Box 865
West Tisbury, MA 02575-0865
phone and fax: 508-683-8594
stamp and crafting supplies

Hot Potatoes
2805 Columbine Place
Nashville, TN 37204
phone: 615-269-8002
fax: 615-269-8004
stamps for fabric and velvet embossing, pp. 62, 65, 91

Loose Ends
P.O. Box 20310
Keizer, OR 97307
phone: 503-390-7457
unique papers and naturals including river cane and bamboo, pp. 48, 130

Magenta
351 Blain
Mont-Saint-Hilaire
Qc J3H 3B4 Canada
phone: 450-446-5253
fax: 450-464-6353
quality rubber stamps and stamp art kits, p. 133

Mainely Shades
100 Gray Road
Falmouth, ME 04105
phone: 1-800-624-6359
lampshades and related materials, p. 52

Michael's Arts & Crafts
See www.michaels.com for store locations
art and craft supplies

Mosaic Mercantile products, p. 97
available from Pearl, Nasco, Michael's and other craft stores

NASCO
phone: 1-800-558-9595
craft concrete, p. 109

Oasis Art & Craft America
Building 2 Unit 1
Homestead Road
Belle Mead, NJ 08502
phone: 908-874-3315
fax: 908-874-5433
Color Shaper® tools, p. 101

Pearl Paint Company
308 Canal Street
New York, NY 10013-2572
phone: 1-800-451-PEARL for catalog
art and craft supplies

Polaroid
Customer Service
phone: 1-800-343-5000
slide film, p. 75

SpotPen
P.O. Box 1559
Las Cruces, NM 88004
phone: 505-523-8820
photo-coloring pens, p. 38

Rockler Woodworking and Hardware
phone: 1-800-279-4441
www.rockler.com
woodworking tools, Danish oil, pins, darkening solution, veneers, and stains, pp. 138, 143

Dawn Anderson
Bloomington, MN

Jane Asper
1357 S. Pennsylvania
Denver, CO 80210
phone: 303-777-3984

Christine Bakholdin
18920 Felbridge Street
Canyon Country, CA
91351
phone: 661-251-0454
artyhands@aol.com

Michael Ball
42A Hedley Street
Maidstone Kent
ME14 5AD UK
phone and fax: 011 44
162-266-1838
freedalepress@cableinet.co.uk

Ann Kegel Bausman
148 Westminster Avenue
Arlington, MA 02474
phone: 781-641-4319
fax: 781-641-7374

Mary E. Becker
Mary Becker Designs
6147 N. Santa Monica
Boulevard
Milwaukee, WI 53217
phone: 414-332-3183
marylamb@execpc.com

Sara E. Burr
Brain Pops
308 Western Avenue, #1
Cambridge, MA 02139
phone: 617-491-7196
brainpops@earthlink.net

Elizabeth Cameron
7 Bloody Brook Rd.
Hampstead, NH 03841

Kathy Cartier
P.O. Box 2422
Park City, UT 84060
phone: 435-649-7087

Cathy A. Cartwright
The Biscuitroot Guild
1649 Hislop Drive
Ogden, UT 84404
phone: 801-627-4309

Paula DeSimone
62 Pleasant Street
Plainville, MA 02762
phone: 508-695-6702

Kathleen Ann Frey
Kathy Frey Designs
24 Harold Street, #3
Somerville, MA 02143
phone: 617-628-4498
kathy_frey@harvard.edu

Lisa Glicksman
400 Sunnyslope Avenue
Oakland, CA 94610
phone: 510-959-8799
lmgdsa@aol.com

Cindy Gorder
5683 E. Pleasant View
Road
Mineral Point, WI 53565
fax: 608-987-3373
gorderdc@mhtc.net

Paula Grasdal
437 Trapelo Road, 2nd
Floor
Belmont, MA 02478
phone: 617-489-4717
pgrasdal@netway.com

Sue Handman
Sue Handman Artware
85 Granite Street
Rockport, MA 01966
phone: 978-546-9435

Kelly A. Henderson
Chameleon Designs
998 N. 1100 West
Farmington, UT 84025
phone: 801-451-7541
fax: 801-451-5410
chameleondesigns@msn.com

Gail Hercher
The Paper Crane
280 Cabot Street
Beverly, MA 01915
phone: 978-927-3131
papergail@aol.com

Susan Jaworski-Stranc
Apple Góer & Prints
Studio
2 Low Street
Newbury, MA 01951
phone: 978-465-9896
stranc@mediaone.net

Maral Kacmichian
Hand Painted Originals
7700 River Road
North Bergen, NJ 07047
phone: 201-662-6200
fax: 201-261-7478

Lisa Kerr
5 Martinwood Road
Jamaica Plain, MA 02130
phone: 617-426-9214

Irene Koronos
Paper Source
1810 Mass Avenue
Cambridge, MA 02140
phone: 617-497-1077

Laura McFadden
49 Vinal Avenue
Somerville, MA 02143
phone: 617-625-7906
pluto4@star.net

Cathy R. McLaurin
Chest
49 High Street
Amesbury, MA 01913
phone: 978-388-5932
candg111@aol.com

Livia McRee
9 Sewall Avenue, #305
Brookline, MA 02446
phone: 617-713-3801
liviamcree@aol.com

Judith G. Miller
Lily's Cottage Designs
P.O. Box 524
Bristol, RI 02809
phone and fax: 401-253-2101
lilyscotdz@aol.com

Lily K. Morris
Star Route 124
Edgartown, MA 02539
phone: 508-627-0894
eelil_27@hotmail.com

Bridgette Newfell
10 Orange Street
Newburyport, MA 01950
phone: 978-465-5969

Laurel Parker
Zeeda Books
20-22 E. 2nd Street
New York, NY 10003
phone: 617-821-6636
zeeda@earthlink.net

Judy Gravett-Player
Player Studios
8 Addison Street
Arlington, MA 02476
phone: 781-646-7108

Anne Russell
8 Lester Terrace
Somerville, MA 02144
phone: 617-629-0769
arussell@exols.com

Peggy Russell
irö Design
450 Harrison Avenue,
Suite 306
Boston, MA 02118
phone and fax:
617-426-3850

Michio Ryan
228 8th Ave. #4
New York, NY 10011

Sandra Salamony
80 Chestnut Street, #4
Cambridge, MA 02139
phone: 617-491-7623
sandranoel@aol.com

Brenda Spitzer
Hand Crafted by Heart
515 South Hale Street
Wheaton, IL 60187
phone: 630-682-8405
fax: 630-682-0218
hcbh@worldnet.att.net

Nikki St. Mary-Kingsley
Geez Louise
41 Court Street
Newton, MA 02460
phone: 617-928-0874
www.geez-louise.com
nik1029@yahoo.com

Elaine Schmidt
Elaine Schmidt Designs
21 Sierra Drive
Califon, NJ 07830
phone: 908-832-2222
fax: 908-832-9108
esdesigns@aol.com

Connie Sheerin
Crafts a la Cart
P.O. Box 246
Lansdowne, PA 01950
phone: 610-626-8162
fax: 610-626-2162
concraft@aol.com

Sarah Stalie
Loose Ends
38 24 River Road North
Keizer, OR 97303
phone: 503-390-7457
fax: 503-390-4724
info@4loosends.com

Lee Strasburger
The Maker of Heavenly
Trousers
95 Clifton Street
Belmont, MA 02478
phone and fax:
617-484-7687

Kelley Tayor
Taylor Design Studio
672 Gateway Drive
Suite 610
Leesburg, VA 02175
phone: 703-443-0825
fax: 703-947-6243

Maria Testa
Designs by Maria
41 Mulberry Circle
Ayer, MA 01432
phone: 978-772-1767

Martha F. Thurlow
Good Ideas
P.O. Box 865
West Tisbury, MA
02575-0805
phone and fax:
508-693-8594

Margaret Tiberio
86 Essex Street, #302
Salem, MA 01970
phone: 978-745-4115

Ellen Wieske
93 Hampshire Street
Cambridge, MA 02139
phone: 617-354-8625
ewcaf@aol.com

Jacqueline Winch
48 Shawine Road
Sandwich, MA 02563
phone: 508-888-6473
jwinch@capecod.net
jacqwinglass@capecod.net

Nancy Worrell
P.O. Box 695
Chapel Hill, NC 27514
phone and fax:
919-967-9309
nowdesigns@aol.com

the authors

Mary Ann Hall is the former editor of *Handcraft Illustrated* magazine. She is currently editor of Craftopia.com, a website devoted to providing artists and crafters with materials, project ideas, and a rich online community.

An art director and writer in Cambridge, Massachusetts, **Sandra Salamony** has designed crafts for many magazines and books.